BREAKING FREE

Breaking Free

WOMEN OF SPIRIT
AT MIDLIFE AND BEYOND

edited by Marilyn Sewell

BEACON
150

BEACON PRESS, BOSTON

Beacon Press
25 Beacon Street
Boston, Massachusetts 02108-2892
www.beacon.org

Beacon Press books
are published under the auspices of
the Unitarian Universalist Association of Congregations.

08 07 06 05 04 8 7 6 5 4 3 2 1

This book is printed on acid-free paper that meets the uncoated paper
ANSI/NISO specifications for permanence as revised in 1992.

Text design by Patricia Duque Campos
Composition by Wilsted & Taylor Publishing Services

Library of Congress Cataloging-in-Publication Data

Breaking free : women of spirit at midlife and beyond /
edited by Marilyn Sewell.—1st ed.
p. cm.
ISBN: 0-8070-2825-8 (pbk. : alk. paper)
1. Spiritual life. 2. Middle aged women—Religious life. I. Sewell, Marilyn.
BL624.B6357 2004
810.8'0382—dc22   2004008571

for Donna

Contents

PART 1: *Necessary Losses*

Time takes from us youth and vigorous health. Relationships falter and shift and are sometimes lost forever. Illness can grab hold and destroy our careless assumptions. "How did we come to be here?" we ask ourselves. And to no one in particular, we ask, "What next?"

PART 2: *Breaking Free*

We come to learn ways that youth could not show us. Moving with a surprising sense of freedom, we break into new territory that is our own. Now our lives and spirits deepen, and we bless the world with what we have become.

BREAKING FREE

Introduction

Around the age of fifty or so, many women begin to loosen from cultural constraints, to become their own persons in ways they perhaps have not dared to do previously. By this time, they begin to become less defined by others and more by their own choices. It is a time rich with possibility for personal and spiritual growth. This book is a collection of essays that witness to that truth.

It is understandable that in our youth both men and women take on certain developmental tasks. We search for a life partner with whom our needs for love and intimacy might be met. We try to figure out how to sustain ourselves financially. But women—for complex reasons of both nature and nurture—are more inclined to relationship as a focus, and men to doing and achieving. Women find that our choices are often determined by the wants and needs of others. Some of us gladly serve, others of us chafe under these roles, still others rebel.

No matter what the circumstance—and in spite of the feminist movement—all too often we have been role-bound as nurturers and caretakers. Our lives become reactive—we respond to the needs of others. An orientation of nurturing is not a bad thing in itself—quite the opposite: dinner is put on the table, children driven to soccer practice, birthday parties given, parents cared for. It's just that in the giving, a woman sometimes loses herself.

When children leave home, women often ask themselves, "What now?" Whether or not we have raised children, we begin to count the years and ask ourselves, "How much time is left? What is pulling at me? What can I yet become?" Those of us who are at all reflective begin to wonder what we have learned in the first half of life that will sustain us and direct us in the second half. Women often come to a deeper sense of self at this time. This movement into personhood does involve some breaking of barriers. There is a kind of release, a kind of freedom, in the breaking and in the choosing. That kind of freedom emerges in the lives of the women whose work is collected here.

These essayists acknowledge, in one way or another, an awareness of their aging, in itself an act of courage. In this youth-oriented society, no one particularly likes to think of themselves as "aging." Growing older is particularly problematic for women: we begin to experience how difficult it is to maintain our equilibrium in a culture that idolizes youth and beauty, and in fact seems unable to conceptualize beauty of person without youth.

But at midlife, inevitably, our bodies will begin to slow and then all too soon to creak and groan like the rigging of a ship that has seen better days. Our intellect loses its keen edge. The youthful blush of flesh goes, and more makeup and "body-shaper" undergarments will fail us at some point. We may begin to ask ourselves a hard question: "If the allure of my youthful body brought me love, will I ever be loved again?"

At this time we are forced into an encounter with the hardest of human realities: we come to understand, not just intellectually but existentially, that we are going to die. It is this acknowledgment of our absolute lack of power over existence, this complete failure to overcome, that invites us into the life of the spirit. It is a necessary and exacting gift. It offers the opportunity to ground ourselves in meaning that goes deeper than the skin. It awakens us and allows us to give deference to the Mystery, to that which we can never grasp and yet which ultimately defines us.

As I did my research, I discovered that there were two basic approaches to writing about aging. One goes something like this: "I'm getting older, and I hate it, and there's nothing I can do about it. It's just awful." The other approach is that of acceptance, of deepening, and a resulting wisdom that can come no other way, I suspect, than in confronting the obvious but elusive fact of one's own mortality. A few very fine writers took the former approach, but no matter how well chosen the words, the results were disappointing. Despair can be interesting in memoir, but to my way of thinking, only if the writer does something with it, is able to move beyond it. And so for the present volume I have chosen writers of the second persuasion, writers who can help women move gracefully and courageously through the second half of their lives.

I must say honestly that finding pieces of writing that deal with spirituality in the mature woman was difficult, and I am moved to ask why. I don't know, I can only surmise. I suspect that writing about one's spiritual life at any age is difficult—but at least in my own experience, the older I get, the less I know, and the more I have to rest in faith. Because I am continually humbled in the face of Mystery, it seems almost arrogant to try to put into words the vastness of which I am beginning to feel a part. To speak, to write, to use words at all is always to narrow and define something as *this* and not *that*, at least in our dualistic culture. To tie words to Spirit is to diminish its power, to deny its Oneness. We search for metaphor, for the old ones have largely lost their power. Or, more often, we simply fall into silence.

Then there is the question of intimacy and revelation. What could be more intimate than one's relationship to the Sacred? That relationship may be too close, too unique and special to reveal to others. We instinctively pull back from such expression, as if to touch it would make it disappear. It's the same reason that writers do not like to speak of their work in progress. As something works its way into our consciousness, it needs space, not definition.

So in most of these pieces, the writers do not hit the subject straight on. What you will find here is testimony about where they have come to, but rarely how they got there. They may not even know. But they have arrived at a place of accepting more deeply who they are, and they are living out of a kind of radical authenticity. In this volume, that is how I'm defining the often used and misused word *spirituality*—a flowering into the person you were meant to be, as you move closer to the Source of Life.

⁓

These personal essays are real, through and through. You will encounter in these pages some of the most honest writing you may yet have come across, for these writers are beyond literary pyrotechnics. They have little interest in dazzling you. Virtually all, however, have a deep interest in getting down and dirty with you about their lives. They have looked at themselves as they are, and life as it is, and they have come to some reconciliation of the two. This is no easy matter, and we are blessed by their willingness to share with us these intimate reflections. Reading their work has informed my living, deepened my spirit.

Breaking Free contains twenty-eight unique voices. These writers have lived long enough and written extensively enough to come to an expression that is their very own, and no other. Visiting with them through their personal stories is like looking at a handful of gemstones, all cut in different forms, all in various sizes and colors, some more complex than others, but all standing in their own particular loveliness and authenticity.

In these pages Susan Griffin tells us how her lifelong activism has shifted to become more compassionate in nature. Ellen Glasgow, near the end of her life, reflects, sums up; among other things, she says, "I have done the work I wished to do for the sake of that work alone. . . ." Alix Shulman reveals how her mother's death made her "fierce with [a] new reality." Audre Lorde shares with us her raw courage as she chooses her own way of meeting the challenge of breast cancer. Erica Jong concludes, "I am old enough to know that laughter, not anger, is the true revelation."

Women can be beautiful at any stage of life. As we age, our aliveness shines forth from the depths of spirit, if we dare to go there. Maturity can bring a sweet kind of joy, as we come to know how deeply connected we are with all that is, as we understand and accept how much we have to give.

I offer these pieces to you as precious gifts from women who have looked boldly at the realities of their lives, have reflected upon these realities, and through their careful telling, have enriched and deepened the lives of their readers. These stories are their legacy and we are the fortunate recipients of their largesse.

PART 1

Necessary Losses

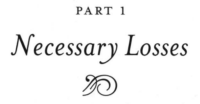

from

Fear of Fifty

ERICA JONG

HE'S FIFTY, SHE'S NOT

At fifty, the last thing I wanted was a public celebration. Three days
before my birthday I took off for a spa in the Berkshires with Molly
(then thirteen)—slept in the same bed with her, giggling before
sleep, slumber party style—worked out all day (as if I were a jock,
not a couch potato), learned trendy low-fat vegetarian recipes, had
my blackheads expunged, my flab massaged, my muscles stretched,
and thought about the second half of my life.

These thoughts alternated between terror and acceptance. Turning fifty, I thought, is like flying: hours of boredom punctuated by
moments of sheer terror.

When, on the evening of my birthday, my husband (who shares
the same birthday but is one year older) arrived, I had to adjust to
the disruption of my woman's world. He liked the food but wise-
cracked about the holistic hokum. His critical-satirical male eye did
not quite ruin my retreat but somehow tainted it. I was doing inner
work in the guise of outer exercise, and his presence made that inner
work harder.

Real men don't like spas.

The year before, when he turned fifty, I had made a party for
him. I sent out invitations that read:

He's fifty.
She's not.
Come help celebrate.

I still couldn't face fifty, so I knew I did not want him to reciprocate for my fiftieth birthday. Nor did I want to do what Gloria Steinem had done: make a public benefit, raise money for women, and rise resplendent in an evening gown, shoulders dusted with glitter—as Gloria's lovely shoulders were—and say: "This is what fifty looks like."

Who can fail to admire such brave affirmation of older women? But I veered between wanting to change the date on my *Who's Who* entry and wanting to move to Vermont and take up organic gardening in drawstring pants and Birkenstocks.

I needed something private, female, and contemplative to sort out these conflicting feelings. A spa was perfect. And my daughter was the perfect companion—despite her adolescent riffing that spares no one, her mother least of all. Still, there is something about a woman turning fifty that is female work, mother-daughter work, not to be shared with the whole male world—or even with those representatives of it whom one loves and cherishes.

My husband and I have always made much of our birthday—in part because we share it and because, having met in midlife, after the wreckage of many relationships, we treasure the synchronicity of our births during World War II, a world of ration coupons and fear of Axis invasions that we only dimly remember from twice-told family tales. One year we took our daughters to Venice—my magic city —another year we made a blast in our new apartment in New York, bought jointly—the ultimate sign of commitment in a world where marriages die like moths.

But fifty is different for a woman than it is for a man. Fifty is a more radical kind of passage to the other side of life, and this was something we could not share. Let him make fun of "new age" contemplation. I needed it, as have women back to antiquity. Venus de Milo contemplates herself turning into the Venus of Willendorf—if she doesn't watch out.

You tell yourself you ought to be beyond vanity. You read feminist books and contemplate falling in love with Alice B. Toklas. But years of brainwashing are not so easy to forget. The beauty trap is deeper than you thought. It's not so much the external pressures as the internal ones that bind. You cannot imagine yourself middle-aged—cute little you who always had "it" even when overweight.

For years I had stayed legally single, fearing both the boredom and the entrapment of something not accidentally called "wedlock"; now I thought the most difficult challenge of all was to keep my mental and spiritual independence while inside a nurturing relationship. This meant constant negotiation of priorities, constant noisy fights, constant struggles for power. If you were lucky enough to feel safe enough to fight and struggle, then you were lucky indeed. If you felt loved enough to scream and yell and exercise your power openly, the marriage had a fifty-fifty chance.

I had come to such a marriage only because I had come to a place where I was not afraid of being alone. I discovered that I liked my own company better than dating. Treasuring my solitude, secure in my ability to provide for myself and my daughter, I suddenly met a soul mate and a friend.

Famous for writing about relationships that flamed with sex then petered out, I surprised myself with this one.

Conversation ignited. The sex was at first disastrous—detumescence at inopportune moments and condoms limply abandoned on the counterpane. So much fear of commitment on both sides that ecstasy seemed irrelevant. Instead, we talked and talked. I found myself liking this person before I knew I loved him—which was in itself a new thrill. I would run away—to California, to Europe—only to call him from far-flung places. We felt our connection so strongly that it seemed we had been together all our lives.

Has anyone dared to write about the disasters of safe sex in the age of AIDS? Has anyone dared to say that most men would rather wear condoms around their necks to ward off the evil eye than put them on their cocks? Has anyone recorded the traumas of midlife lovers who have been through everything from fifties technical virginity to sixties sexual gluttony to seventies health and fitness (you met your lovers at Nautilus Clubs) to eighties decadence (long limousines and short dresses and men who impersonated Masters of the Universe) to nineties terror of AIDS warring with natural horniness?

And then there are the eternal questions of love and sex: Can there be friendship between men and women as long as the hormones rage and rule? How is sex related to love—and love to sex? Are we truly pigeonholed in our sexuality—or does society alone insist on this? What is "straight"? What is "gay"? What is "bi"? And does any of it matter deep in one's soul? Shouldn't we get rid of these labels in an attempt to be really open to ourselves and to each other?

What was happening to me in the second part of my life? I was getting myself back and I liked that self. I was getting the humor, the intensity, the balance I had known in childhood. But I was getting it back with a dividend. Call it serenity. Call it wisdom. I knew what mattered and what did not. Love mattered. Instant orgasm did not.

I look around me at fifty and see the women of my generation coping with getting older. They are perplexed, and the answer to their perplexity is not another book on hormones. The problem goes deeper than menopause, face-lifts, or whether to fuck younger men. It has to do with the whole image of self in a culture in love with youth and out of love with women as human beings. We are terrified at fifty because we do not know what on earth we can become when we are no longer young and cute. As at every stage of our lives, there are no role models for us. Twenty-five years of feminism (and backlash), then feminism again—and we still stand at the edge of an abyss. What to become now that our hormones have let us go?

At fifty, the madwoman in the attic breaks loose, stomps down the stairs, and sets fire to the house. She won't be imprisoned anymore. The second wave of anger is purer than the first. Suddenly the divisions between women don't matter. Old or young, brown or white, gay or straight, married or un-, poor or rich—we are all discriminated against just because we are women. And we won't go back to the old world of injustice. We can't. It's too late.

The anger of midlife is a ferocious anger. In our twenties, with success and motherhood still before us, we could imagine that something would save us from second-classness—either achievement or marriage or motherhood. Now we know that nothing can save us. We have to save ourselves.

Fifty is the time when time itself begins to seem short. The sense of time running out has been exacerbated lately by the AIDS epidemic and the deaths of so many friends still in their thirties, forties, and fifties. Who knows whether there will be a better time? The time is always now.

At nineteen, at twenty-nine, at thirty-nine, even—goddess help me—at forty-nine, I believed that a new man, a new love, a move, a change to another city, another country, would somehow change my inner life.

Not so now.

I know that my inner life is my own achievement whether there is a partner in my life or not. I know that another mad, passionate love affair would be only a temporary distraction—even if "temporary" means two or three years. I know that my soul is what I have to nurture and develop and that, alone or with a partner, the problems of climbing your own mountain are not so very different.

In a relationship, you still require autonomy, separateness, privacy. Outside a relationship, you still need self-love and self-esteem.

I write this book from a place of self-acceptance, cleansing anger, and raucous laughter.

I am old enough to know that laughter, not anger, is the true revelation.

Facing

DOROTHY WALL

On an *Oprah* show about weddings, a celebrity appeared with her daughter to regale viewers with the extravagant details of her daughter's wedding: gold-embroidered napkins; jewel-strung dress; dense, velvet stands of roses and tulips as if out of a Renaissance oil painting. I found myself watching like the outsider we all are to celebrity lives, fascinated and appalled. (Over three million dollars for a wedding when the fourth graders my daughter teaches are virtually without books!)

As mother, daughter, and Oprah gushed, I was struck by the celebrity's face. Sitting next to her daughter, who looked like a regular person, this woman looked not like a mother but a caricature of her younger self, her skin so face-lift taut as to be masklike, eyes weighted with mascara, blond pageboy that fit like a helmet. She made me think of a Marcel Marceau mime routine in which a man is stuck in a laughing mask. He makes a great effort to pull it off, heaving and staggering around the stage, but can't dislodge it. The audience laughs at his antics, seeing only his laughing face, while underneath the mask the man is crying. No one can see his pain. He is caught in his solitude, alone with what he feels, unrecognized.

This woman's face had become that mask, a smiling reproduction of youth, divorced from the self inside. It made me sad, evoking echoes of Dickens's Miss Havisham sitting for decades in her moldering wedding dress, waiting for her groom who never arrives. Unable to arrest the moment of youthful ardor and anticipation, Miss Havisham arrests only the props around her, and even they decay until she is jilted by time as much as by love. For all its careful preservation, this celebrity's face, like that yellowed wedding dress, was a costume that with each passing year would be less matched to the person inside.

Those who have face-lifts may think they have preserved their faces. In fact, they have been defaced, the marks of a life removed, the blemishes, the idiosyncrasies. We think of defacing as spoiling what was originally pristine, perfect. This defacing is the opposite: it attempts to restore perfection by stripping a face of what is personal, singular. To be defaced is to lose part of the self, our individual expression.

The promise of the reconstructed face is not just that it will be eternally young or perfect, but that it is reproducible. If it can be made for celebrities it can be made for others, the same high cheekbones, taut skin. We can mold a face, make it as art object, manipulate it, change it. We can do it for you. The face has become a consumer product, an exchangeable commodity. It can be both discarded and acquired, an emblem of commerce and exchange. Familiar terrain for women. To reclaim our natural face is to step out of this commercial landscape.

After the *Oprah* show I was compelled to dig up and pin above my desk an old postcard/photo of artist Georgia O'Keeffe, standing in the desert like a tree. O'Keeffe's face is turned away from the camera, unconcerned with the viewer. She gazes into the distance as if focused on an inner vision and the grandeur of the desert around her at the same time. Her face is lined, stolid, implacable, like photos of Indian warriors. There is no artifice, no cover, no disjunction between face and self. She is not smiling, neither does she appear sad. She radiates strength and self-possession, a word she embodies: to literally possess the self, to not be apart from who you are.

If the cover-up of the aging face, as Jungian psychologist James Hillman and others contend, acts to discourage the revelation of character, then a face left bare is a revealing marker of a life. It is precisely this exposure that produces the urge to disguise. What if our face shows sadness, strain, fatigue—or worse, our own fragility and decay, no longer a perfect surface. So what, O'Keeffe says. This is the whole of who I am.

In a remarkable statement about the trap of perfection, actress Heddy Lamarr lamented in her 1966 autobiography, *Ecstacy and Me*, "My face has been my misfortune. . . . My face is a mask I cannot remove. I must always live with it. I curse it." A woman of intelligence and humor, she felt confined by a public perception that equated her self with her beautiful face. How ironic and sad that other women work hard to reproduce that confinement.

To don the mask of perfection reinforces a narrow definition of beauty and acceptability that will heighten, not dissipate our anxieties about age. The artificial and ultimately futile attempt to stop our natural progression into age is an act of self-abandonment. We become like both Marceau's audience, who can't see, and the man behind the laughing mask, who is trapped: we're unable to see how we're trapped in our own effort.

To face: to meet or confront squarely. To confront with boldness, courage. Facing: to turn the face in a specified direction. Like many people, I track my loss of youth with the eyes of the amazed inner self struggling to adjust. But I hope I'll have the courage to face my aging with curiosity, amusement, pride, and equanimity, and to confront boldly or turn away from the viewer's gaze. Like O'Keeffe, I want to draw my gaze from within and focus it outward on the astounding world around me.

Sink or Swim

ANNICK SMITH

Indian summer. Montana. Rivers. You get the picture. Sky-blue waters gurgling with trout. Freckled cottonwood leaves like a yellow flotilla. Kingfishers, rose hips, purple asters. For me, eye-popping, soul-singing joy if that river is the Big Blackfoot a few miles upstream from my house.

By late afternoon on such a day, desk work is impossible. The river calls to me—a cathedral bell ringing—and I must go to it. The air is dry, hot, and blue, and the topsoil along the bluff is fluffy, like powder. As I walk my dogs up the Blackfoot from Whitaker Bridge, I turn my eyes from logged-off hills down to the cleft gorge where the snake of bright waters unwinds.

I am walking under ponderosa pines, trailing my fingers along reddish columns of picture-puzzle bark. The river is splattered with yellow light, but the water runs green. The Big Blackfoot is green as the scent of rain. Green as frogs and moss and evergreen trees. I crush pine needles under my feet, and their perfume mingles with the sharp odor of cottonwood sap and the trout scent of water over stones. Larches shower needles of gold on my head. These are the days of gold. I will dream of them during winter nights, the cold that may pounce, perhaps tomorrow, like a cougar from this self-same forest.

Betty Boop, my big-eyed shepherd dog, and Little Red, a bouncy young fellow part chow, part golden retriever, race ahead on the trail of a squirrel. Summer tourists are gone, only one jeep in the parking area. We head for a sandy beach that cuddles between arms of stone across from a great cracked tower of red rock. The rose-pink slabs rise like a Moorish castle above a tree-shaded pool.

I am sweating. The pool is inviting. I decide to take the last plunge of summer. But there on my beach, stretched out like a walrus on an aluminum lounge, is a huge naked man. He basks in rays of the sinking sun, and as my dogs sniff at his toes he raises a listless hand, turns his head toward me, waves.

I call my dogs and flee. Moving quickly through patches of poison ivy invasive as the nudist, I climb over a rocky headland, descend a fisherman's trail to a peninsula of silver-tossed willows. Betty and Red rush into the willows. There is a thrashing noise—a whitetail buck leaps from the brush and into the river. I watch him swim into the dappled current, head high, antlers gilded with sunlight. Buck. Naked. I laugh at the pure surprising coincidence. An osprey dives from the sky.

My dogs bark. They are barking at a raft with four people that is bobbing toward us from a bend in the river. Fishing lines extend on each side, like glowing cobwebs.

"How's it going?" I shout.

"Pretty good," says one fellow.

"Gorgeous day," says a girl.

"Anyone upstream?" I ask.

"No. I think we're the last."

Good, I think, for I know there's another swimming hole just ahead. My bank lies in shadows, but on the opposite shore a huge rock stack catches the light, its striated face patterned chartreuse and orange with lichens. At its feet is a sunny, graveled beach. This will be my perfect, private island.

When the raft is out of sight I strip off my shorts and T-shirt, leaving on my underpants and Tevas, and begin to ford the river. Ankle deep, the water is not too cold, but as I wade to my thighs it turns icy. I catch my breath. This is foolish. I should turn back, but I plunge in. I'm a strong swimmer. I have swum this river many days. But never in October. Never so alone. Never over sixty.

The current is stronger than it looks. I kick hard, turn my arms like windmills until I find myself in slower water. I crawl over slick stones—aqua, maroon, green—shivering toward shore. Although the sun still tips the great lichened rock and the pebbled beach holds the day's heat, I am cold, exposed, a half-naked crazy old woman clutching her arms around her flabby stomach, her breasts. My dogs have followed. They spray me with water, wag their tails.

Light is draining out of the canyon, so I don't linger. Going back I'll be smarter, I think. I will make my way upstream, then let the current carry me to the home shore, to my dry clothes, safety and warmth. But I've forgotten that the river is low. Slime-covered stones extend far into shallow water before the current takes over. I'm crawling crabwise again. And when I reach the deep water, it doesn't ride me homeward but curves downriver to the pool where I started my up-stream journey.

I'm winded before I get halfway across. I kick and stroke, kick and stroke, going nowhere fast. My breath comes in gasps; the quickened beat of my heart pounds in my ears. Fear finds me. Not fear of drowning, but fear that my strength will fail and I will be vulnerable as a leaf, at the mercy of the river. Pull harder, I instruct my arms. My arms obey.

When I break through the current into a safe eddy, goose bumps cover my flesh; long white hair plasters my face; water drips from my eyes like tears. I stumble toward my clothes, the dogs frolicking and nosing at my weak knees. Even dressed and standing in a patch of sun, I tremble with the knowledge of mortality. I am older and weaker than the person I imagined I was, cold to the bone. Get moving, I tell myself. Get your blood running.

I start walking upriver on a piney ledge toward Belmont Creek. My head aches. My feet drag. It will take an hour before I feel halfway normal.

A mile ahead I see a jumble of sticks on a tall snag—the bald eagle aerie on Goose Flats. A white-headed giant screams at me as he glides from his perch. I want to scream back, "Hey, you, I'm still alive too!"

Here is what I learned from that Indian-summer Blackfoot plunge. Take no chances when you are dealing with a wild and precious river. Stay humble. The river is wider than it seems. Respect it. Death waits under slime-covered stones. Every living thing is mortal.

What This Old Hand Knows

ALMA ROBERTS GIORDAN

My husband of fifty-five years kissed my hand. I withdrew it in embarrassment. After all, he was never that demonstrative even in our courting days. "It's not a very pretty hand," I explained, passing the fruit bowl. "To me it is," he insisted.

I looked at my hand with candor. No, it wasn't at all pretty. And yet, it was fair and good to me. Gratefully I examined its five practical digits. (Most of my peers always had graceful "piano fingers.") Slowly I began to appreciate what this hand had been able to accomplish in response to my lifetime demands. For all my deprecation, it bore me no malice, not even a twinge in an overburdened knuckle.

How many microcosmic worlds has it moved about, naked of glove, as it urged beauty and food from a cooperative earth? How many fragile seedlings has it encouraged to fruition? How many tears has it wiped away with balled fist, or offered a paper tissue to another? How many Band-Aids has it applied to generations of minor abrasions? Questions. Answers.

This square hand still wears a thin gold band between a tiny diamond and family ring. Its nails are short, with deep half-moons. Wrinkles, testaments of eighty years, characterize it, with a scattering of freckles and liver spots, along a network of prominent veins. It certainly is not a pretty hand. But it has served me well—turning pages, picking blueberries, tossing salad, braiding a child's hair. It is everything to the old cat, who eagerly awaits the food and drink I provide. It has combed burrs out of hunting dogs' tails and extended fingers to blue budgies for convenient perches. It has rescued turtles, crickets, sparrows, and garter snakes from dry wells.

For how many years has this hand and its mate mounted the keyboard of a trusty typewriter, pounding out letters that become words that eventually filled drawers with poems, essays, and stories without complaint as to the worth of such mileage? And this but one more facet of my old hand's dexterity.

And so I proclaim it a wondrous hand, such a miracle, as Walt Whitman and others have acknowledged. To have filtered sunlight, caught fireflies, tested daisies for "he-loves-me, he-loves-me-not," held buttercups under a child's chin, and triggered jewelweed seeds into tomorrow is no slight accomplishment for any member. To have mastered a tugging knife, then released it, is a great piece of work for so humble a servant. How dexterous you are, Hand, I tell it, to dial a phone, crack a nut, catch a ball, push a swing, sew a seam, turn a wheel, apply a brake, feel textures of flesh and fabric, and sign my name.

To have grasped other hands in greeting or prayer or farewell, waved loved ones off, smoothed a beloved husband's brow as he entered eternity: Blest have you been, old Hand. To have stroked a long-needled pine bough, held a lens over a moth's wing—such experiences should never be discounted. O good and faithful Hand, I repeat, let me remember the fine things you've done. Here's water, here's soap to wash away deeds less than noble. Luxuriate in its cleansing joy. Here's food to maneuver to mouth, to the flesh and blood of me, to achieve growth and fulfillment.

Here's a key to unlock the door, a shell to hold to an ear, sand to sift, kindling to lay on a fire, a small torch to carry. Here's a knob, a switch, a button, a zipper, a bell, a guitar with strings to twang.

Here's a nail to pound into a wall on which a memory may be hung in exultation, praise, and thanksgiving. O Hand, you truly are exceedingly beautiful and worthy of recognition. Bless the faithful heart of the spouse who also found you so, and kissed your telltale lifeline.

from

Fierce Attachments

VIVIAN GORNICK

The years are coming up thickly. . . forty-six, forty-seven, forty-eight. . . There is no past now, only the ongoing present. . . seventy-eight, seventy-nine, eighty. Eighty. My God, my mother is eighty. We stand still, looking at each other. She shrugs her shoulder and sits down on the couch in her living room.

She came to my house this afternoon. We had a drink, then went out to dinner in the neighborhood, then I walked her home. She made coffee and we talked, looked at pictures, some old (America, 1941), some older (Russia, 1913), and we read together from a batch of letters we have dipped into fifty times in my life; letters written to her in 1922 by one Noah Shecter, formerly a professor of literature in Rumania and at the time of the letter-writing manager of the bakery where my mother worked as a bookkeeper. The letters are remarkable: nineteenth-century romantic fantasy written by a lonely man living in the Bronx with an unintellectual wife and three needy children, his head filled with Ibsen, Gorki, Mozart, writing his heart out each night at midnight to a vain brown-eyed empty vessel of receptivity (my eighteen-year-old mother) who would read these impassioned outpourings at eight in the morning before she went off to work to see the man who had written them stiff and formal in a high starched collar, looking like Franz Kafka in the insurance company.

Now, sixty years later, I hold these hundreds of yellowed sheets covered with thickly scrawled European handwriting, the black ink long ago turned brown, and read of Noah Shecter's midnight desperation that my mother should understand how full his heart is, just having seen Ibsen's *Brand* performed in a Fourteenth Street theater, and how necessary it is that he let her know how well the actors captured the essential meaning of this very great play. The letters and the pictures surround us (I see her as she must have looked when she first read them)—fragments, scraps, tales told and retold of the life lived and the life unlived. Especially the one unlived.

A sad, silent weight hangs about my mother all evening. She looks very pretty tonight—soft white hair, soft smooth skin, the wrecked face looking wonderfully whole again—but the years are dragging inside her, and in her eyes I see the confusion, the persistent confusion.

"A lifetime gone by," she says quietly.

My pain is so great I dare not feel it. "Exactly," I say evenly. "Not lived, just gone by."

The softness in her face hardens into definition. She looks at me and, with iron in her voice, says in Yiddish, "So you'll write down: From the beginning it was all lost."

We sit together then, silent, not embroiled with each other, two women only staring into the obscurity of all that lost life. My mother looks neither young nor old, only deeply absorbed by the terribleness of what she is seeing. I do not know how I look to her.

We always walked, she and I. We don't always walk now. We don't always argue, either. We don't always do any of the things we always did. There is no always anymore. The fixed patterns are beginning to break up. This breakup has its own pleasures and surprises. In fact, surprise is now the key word between us. We cannot depend on change, but we can depend on surprise. However, we cannot always depend on surprise, either. This keeps us on our toes.

I come to see her one night with an old friend of mine, a man who grew up with me, someone we've both known for thirty years. I say "known" advisedly. This man is something of a lunatic. An inspired lunatic, to be sure, but a lunatic nonetheless. He, like Davey Levinson, is educated in a vacuum, and he speaks a kind of imaginative gibberish. It is the only way he knows how to get through the ordinary anxiety of the ordinary day.

We are having coffee and cake. I am eating too much cake. I am, in fact, wolfing down the cake. My mother is getting crazy, watching me. She cries, "Stop it! For God's sake, stop eating like that. Don't you care at all that you'll gain two pounds and hate yourself tomorrow? Where's your motivation?"

My friend, sitting at the table beside me, his head thrust forward and down and twisted to the side, looking at her like the madman that he is, starts going on nonsensically about motivation. "You know, of course, that motivation is life," he says. "Life itself. Taken from the Latin *motus,* it means to move, set in motion, engage. . . ."

My mother looks at him. I can see in her face that she does not understand the construction of these sentences. She feels put down: if she doesn't understand something she is being told she is stupid. Her expression becomes one of glittering scorn. "You think you're telling me something I don't know?" she says. "You think I was born yesterday?" No surprise here.

One week later I'm sitting in her apartment drinking tea with her, and from out of nowhere she says to me, "So tell me about your abortion." She knows I had an abortion when I was thirty, but she has never referred to it. I, in turn, know she had three abortions during the Depression, but I never mention them, either. Now, suddenly. . . . Her face is unreadable. I don't know what has stirred the inquiry and I don't know what to tell her. Should I tell her the truth or. . . ? What the hell. The truth. "I had an abortion with my legs up against the wall in an apartment on West Eighty-eighth Street, with Demerol injected into my veins by a doctor whose consulting room was the corner of Fifty-eighth Street and Tenth Avenue." She nods at me as I speak, as though these details are familiar, even expected. Then she says, "I had mine in the basement of a Greenwich Village nightclub, for ten dollars, with a doctor who half the time when you woke up you were holding his penis in your hand." I look at her in admiration. She has matched me clause for clause, and raised the ante with each one. We both burst out laughing at the same moment. Surprise.

Yet another night I am sitting at her table and we are talking of the time she went to work when I was eight years old. This is a story I never tire of hearing.

"What made you decide to do it, Ma? I mean, why that time rather than any other?"

"I always wanted to work, always. God, how I loved having my own money in my pocket! It was the middle of the war, you threw a stone you got seven jobs, I couldn't resist."

"So what did you do?"

"I read the want ads one morning and I got dressed, took the subway downtown, and applied for a job. In ten minutes I had it. What was the name of that company? I've forgotten it now."

"Angelica Uniform Company," I instantly supply.

"You remember!" She smiles beatifically at me. "Look at that. She remembers. I can't remember. She remembers."

"I am the repository of your life now, Ma."

"Yes, you are, you are. Let's see now. Where were we?"

"You went downtown and got the job."

"Yes. So I came home and told Papa, 'I have a job.'"

"How did he respond?"

"Badly. Very badly. He didn't want me to work. He said, 'No other wife in the neighborhood works, why should you work.' I said, 'I don't care what any other wife in the neighborhood does, I want to work.'" She stares into this memory, shaking her head. Her voice falters. "But it was no good, no good. I didn't last long."

"Eight months," I say.

"Yes, eight months."

"Why, Ma? Why only eight months?"

"Papa was miserable. He kept saying to me, 'The children need you.'"

"That was silly," I interrupt. "I remember being *excited* that you were working. I loved having a key around my neck and rushing home every afternoon to do things that made it easier for you."

"Then he said, 'You're losing weight.'"

"You were twenty pounds overweight. It was *great* that you were losing weight."

"What can I tell you?" she says to me. "Either you were going to make a hell in the house or you were going to be happy. I wanted to be happy. He didn't want me to work. I stopped working."

We are quiet together for a while. Then I say, "Ma, if it was now, and Papa said he didn't want you to work, what would you do?"

She looks at me for a long moment. She is eighty years old. Her eyes are dim, her hair is white, her body is frail. She takes a swallow of her tea, puts down the cup, and says calmly, "I'd tell him to go fuck himself."

Real surprise.

We're in the Lincoln Center library for a Saturday afternoon concert. We've arrived late and all the seats are taken. We stand in the darkened auditorium leaning against the wall. I start to worry. I know my mother cannot stand for two and a half hours. "Let's go," I whisper to her. "Sh-h-h," she says, pushing the air away with her hand. I look around. In the aisle seat next to me is a little boy, tossing about on his seat. Beside him his young mother. Next to her another little boy, and next to him the husband and father. The woman lifts the little boy in the aisle seat onto her lap and motions my mother to sit down. My mother leans over, gives the woman her most brilliant smile, and says coyly, "When you'll be eighty, and you'll want a seat at a concert, I'll come back and give you one." The woman is charmed. She turns to her husband to share her pleasure. Nothing doing. He stares balefully at my mother. Here is one Jewish son who hasn't forgotten. His response pulls me up short, reminds me of how seductive my mother has always been, how unwilling she is to part with this oldest trick of the trade, how dangerous and untrustworthy is this charm of hers.

On and on it goes. My apartment is being painted. I spend two nights on her couch. Whenever I sleep over I like to make the coffee in the morning, because she has gotten used to weak coffee and I like mine strong. Meanwhile, she has become convinced that her weak coffee is the correct way to make coffee, and although she has said to me, "All right, you don't like my coffee, make it yourself," she stands over me in the kitchen and directs me to make it as she makes it.

"It's enough already," she says as I spoon coffee into the pot.

"No, it's not," I say.

"It *is*. For God's sake, enough!"

"Look for yourself, Ma. See how far short of the measuring line it is?"

She looks. The evidence is indisputable. There is not enough coffee in the pot. She turns away from me, the flat edge of her hand cutting the air in that familiar motion of dismissal.

"Ah, leave me alone," she says in deep trembling disgust.

I stare at her retreating back. That dismissiveness of hers: it will be the last thing to go. In fact, it will never go. It is the emblem of her speech, the idiom of her being, that which establishes her in her own eyes. The dismissal of others is to her the struggle to rise from the beasts, to make distinctions, to know the right and the wrong of a thing, to not think it unimportant, ever, that the point be made. Suddenly her life presses on my heart.

We are each less interested in justice than we used to be. The antagonism between us is no longer relentless. We have survived our common life, if not together at least in each other's presence, and there is a peculiar comradeship between us now. But the habit of accusation and retaliation is strong, so our conversation is slightly mad these days.

"What I've lived through," my mother will sigh.

"You haven't lived through *any*thing," I will retort.

"You have some damned nerve," she will shout, "to say that to me."

Silence. Anger. Separation.

Unexpectedly, her face clears and she says, "You know what farmer cheese costs now? You wouldn't believe it. Two-fifty-eight a pound."

And I'm willing, I'm willing. When I see the furious self-pity vanish from her face I allow my own to evaporate. If in the middle of a provocative exchange she says, "Well, that's the mother you got, it would have been better with another one, too damned bad this is the one you got," and I nod, "You can say that again," we both start laughing at the same time. Neither one of us, it seems, wishes to remain belligerent one sentence longer than the other. We are, I think, equally amazed that we have lived long enough to be responsive for whole minutes at a time simply to being in the world together, rather than concentrating on what each of us is or is not getting from the other.

But it has no staying power, this undreamed-of equanimity. It drifts, it gets lost, flashes up with unreliable vibrancy, then refuses to appear when most needed, or puts in an appearance with its strength much reduced. The state of affairs between us is volatile. Flux is now our daily truth. The instability is an astonishment, shot through with mystery and promise. We are no longer nose to nose, she and I. A degree of distance has been permanently achieved. I glimpse the joys of detachment. This little bit of space provides me with the intermittent but useful excitement that comes of believing I begin and end with myself.

It is August: New York under siege. A mountain of airless heat presses down on the streets of the city. Not a bit of summer sensuality in this heat. This heat is only oppressive.

Yesterday I sat with a friend drinking iced tea in Paley Park, recovering for a moment from the exhaustion of the day. The wall of rushing water behind us created a three-sided courtyard of miraculous cool. We gazed out at the street shimmering only fifty feet from where we sat.

My friend and I, usually quite talkative, spoke listlessly of this and that: projected work, work in hand, a movie he had seen, a book I was reading, a mutual friend's new love affair. I thought I had been equally responsive to all of our small talk, but then my friend said to me, "You're remarkably uninterested in men."

"Why do you say that?" I asked.

"Every other woman I know, or man for that matter, if they've been without as long as you have, it's on their minds constantly. First priority. Not you. You seem never to think about it."

As he spoke I saw myself lying on a bed in late afternoon, a man's face buried in my neck, his hand moving slowly up my thigh over my hip, our bodies striped with bars of hot light coming through the window blinds. The image burned through me in seconds. I felt stunned by loss: the fun and sweetness of love, the deliciousness, the shimmer. I swallowed hard on empty air.

"No," I said. "I guess I don't."

⸺

Life is difficult: a glory and a punishment. Ideas are excitement, glamorous company. Loneliness eats into me. When the balance between struggle and self-pity is maintained, I feel myself one of the Odd Women—that is, I see myself on a continuum of that amazing two-hundred-year effort—and I am fortified, endowed with new spirit, new will. When the balance is lost, I feel buried alive in failure and deprivation, without love or connection. Friendships are random, conflicts prevail, work is the sum of its disabilities.

Tonight I am hanging on by my fingernails, barely able to hold it all together. I sit at my mother's kitchen table, drinking coffee. We have just eaten dinner. She stands at the sink washing her dishes. We are both edgy tonight. "It's the heat," she says. The apartment is air-conditioner cool, but we both love real air too much. We have turned off the machine and opened the window. For a minute the crowded noisy avenue down below invades the room, but very quickly its rush subsides into white noise, background buzz. We return almost without a pause to our own restless gloom.

My mother is conversant with all that is on my mind. She is also familiar with the usual order of my litany of complaint: work, friends, money. This evening, yesterday's conversation in Paley Park seems to drift in the window on the sexy summer air, and to my own surprise I find myself saying, "It *would* be nice to have a little love right now."

I expect my mother to laugh and say, "What's with you tonight?" Instead, not even looking up from the dishes, she goes on automatic and says to me, "Well, now perhaps you can have a little sympathy for *me*."

I look up slowly at her. "What?" I say. I'm not sure I have heard right. "What was that you said?"

"I said maybe you can understand *now* what my life was like when Papa died. What it's been like all these years. Now that you're suffering from the absence of love yourself, maybe you can understand."

I stare at her. I stare and I stare. Then I'm up from the table, the cup is falling over, I fly against the kitchen wall, a caged animal. The pot she's washing clatters into the sink.

"What the hell are you talking about?" I shout. "What *are* you talking about? Again love? And yet again love? Am I never to hear anything but love from you until I die? Does my life mean nothing to you? Absolutely nothing?"

She stands at the sink rigid with terror, her eyes fixed on me, her lips white, the color draining from her face. I think I'm giving her a heart attack, but I can't stop.

"It is true," I rage on, my voice murderous now with the effort to keep it down. "I've not been successful. Neither at love, nor at work, nor at living a principled life. It is also true I made no choices, took no stands, stumbled into my life because I was angry and jealous of the world beyond my reach. But *still!* Don't I get any credit for spotting a good idea, Ma? That one should *try* to live one's life? Doesn't that count, Ma? That counts for nothing, Ma?"

Her fear dissolves into pity and regret. She's so pliable these days, it's heartbreaking. "No, no," she protests, "it's another world, another time. I didn't mean anything. Of *course* you get credit. All the credit in the world. Don't get so excited. I was trying to sympathize. I said the wrong thing. I don't know how to talk to you anymore."

Abruptly, the rush of words in her is halted. Another thought has attracted her attention. The line of defense swerves. "Don't you see?" she begs softly. "Love was all I had. What did I have? I had nothing. *Nothing*. And what was I *going* to have? What *could* I have? Everything you say about your life is true, I understand how true, but you have had your work, you *have* your work. And you've traveled. My God, you've traveled! You've been halfway around the world. What wouldn't I have given to travel! I had only your father's love. It was the only sweetness in my life. So I loved his love. What could I have done?"

But mutual heartbreak is not our style. "That's not good enough, Ma," I say. "You were forty-six when he died. You could have gone out into life. Other women with a lot less at their disposal did. You *wanted* to stay inside the idea of Papa's love. It's crazy! You've spent thirty years inside the idea of love. You could have had a life."

Here the conversation ends. She is done with pleading. Her face hardens. She draws herself up into remembered inflexibility. "So," she reverts to Yiddish, the language of irony and defiance. "You'll write down here on my tombstone: From the very beginning it was all water under the bridge."

She turns from the dishes in the sink, wipes her hands carefully on a towel, and walks past me into the living room. I stand in the kitchen looking down at the patterned linoleum on the floor, but then after a while I follow. She is lying stretched out on the couch, her arm across her forehead. I sink down into a chair not far from the couch. This couch and this chair are positioned as they were in the living room in the Bronx. It is not difficult to feel that she has been lying on this couch and I have been sitting in this chair almost the whole of our lives.

We are silent. Because we are silent the noise of the street is more compelling. It reminds me that we are not in the Bronx, we are in

Manhattan: the journey has been more than a series of subway stops for each of us. Yet tonight this room is so like that other room, and the light, the failing summer light, suddenly it seems a blurred version of that other pale light, the one falling on us in the foyer.

My mother breaks the silence. In a voice remarkably free of emotion—a voice detached, curious, only wanting information—she says to me, "Why don't you go already? Why don't you walk away from my life? I'm not stopping you."

I see the light, I hear the street. I'm half in, half out.

"I know you're not, Ma."

from

A Good Enough Daughter

ALIX KATES SHULMAN

A year after my mother died, *Memoirs of an Ex-Prom Queen*, which had once scandalized my hometown, was reissued in a twenty-fifth-anniversary edition that took me back to Cleveland for some readings. As I had an extra hour before the rental car was due back at the airport and it was a brilliant May Sunday morning, I decided to drive past the Shaker house once more.

As I slowed to a stop, I was shocked to see how much had changed in the few months since my parents had left the world: a winter storm had taken down the last remaining elm, leaving the great lawn bare; the wooden trim, most of which Dad had kept brown, a color that requires infrequent painting, was now white; and the entire house was crowned with a shimmering new roof.

Unable to tear myself away, I parked the car and walked up the drive. A giant middle-aged man came around the house to meet me. He wore overalls and carried a trowel. "Is there something I can do for you?" he said in a forbidding British accent. "Doctor?" I replied, thrusting out my hand and introducing myself as the daughter of the former owners. Instead of apologizing for my Sunday intrusion and retreating down the drive, I waited to be invited inside, as Mom would have done.

The doctor kindly complied. He took me on a tour of the house, proudly displaying all the work that he and his wife had done. The carpets were gone, revealing pristine hardwood floors. The kitchen was in the process of being stripped and renovated. The back entrance had been repositioned near the porch and the kitchen door sealed off. The summer porch had been winterized. Upstairs, Mom's closet had been captured to make space for a Jacuzzi in the adjacent bathroom, and her dressing room/studio converted to a closet. My grandmother's rooms over the garage, originally built as servants' quarters, were now offices for the doctor's wife. Electronic devices enhanced every room. The vast third floor had been transformed into a gym with all the latest exercise equipment. All the walls had been repainted lively colors: the living room a designer pink, the hallways pale rose, the bedrooms green, blue, lavender, and cream. The biggest surprise was the room I'd always slept in—now a cheerful nursery for the doctor's new baby, with stenciled walls, a crib, a bassinet, and a veritable menagerie of stuffed animals.

At first sight my eyes revolted at the changes, as if my parents' pasts were being violated, their memory destroyed. Lucky for them, I thought, not to see their home desecrated by strangers.

Then I remembered Mom saying that if she were to do it again she would furnish the house differently—not with antiques but in a contemporary style. She would probably approve of the changes (she'd certainly applaud the new kitchen), and Dad wouldn't care one way or another, as long as he didn't have to foot the bill.

"You need only claim the events of your life to make yourself yours. When you truly possess all you have been and done, which may take some time, you are fierce with reality," wrote the octogenarian playwright Florida Scott-Maxwell.

As I followed the doctor back down the stairs, a memorial I'd recently attended for a friend's mother flashed to mind. To the assembled mourners my friend had described waking up one morning shortly after his mother's death, inexplicably full of joy. "I couldn't understand it," he said. "There I was, a man who had just lost his mother—and yet I was happy. How could this be?" And not only happy, he said; he was filled with a prodigious rush of energy. Then he understood that when he'd opened his eyes that morning his mother's presence had entered him. Somehow she had infused him with her energy and washed him with happiness. From then on, he said, he was never without her.

I recognized that what my friend described was Scott-Maxwell's fierce jolt of reality. How often it now came over me: each time I opened my father's pocket watch to check the hour or brazenly wore my mother's mink; in fact, whenever I looked into the mirror. Having so long defined myself by our difference, I would once have cringed to see my parents' faces looking out at me. But now, when we are as distinct as life and death, it pleases me. Hearing Mom's easy laughter in my throat, feeling Dad's gestures in my hands, sur-rounded in my New York loft by their effects—the cloisonné honey-moon lamp, the framed portrait of Bob, Dad's crystal owl, Mom's Nevelson, and, yes, my stick of Wrigley's Spearmint gum—I know better who I am. The powers those objects embody, which I've fed upon since birth—Mom's sensuality and will, Dad's rationality and focus—are, like my parents themselves, the source of what I am.

But who were they? Though I've squinted through the keyhole at their past, read their private letters and manuscripts, I still can't say. Not only because my self-regard kept me ignorant of their lives but because like every parent they presented personae designed to pro-tect now their children, now themselves. My deepest knowledge of them is as biased, partial, and self-serving as my knowledge of my brother, Bob. The documents I hoped would reveal them to me con-firmed their energy and optimism but kept their secrets. How could it be otherwise? How can one peer through the windows of one's parents' lives without encountering one's own opaque reflection?

As the doctor led me out the back door through the garden (where he'd been digging up Mom's roses to replant near the garage), I got a strong whiff of Mom's lilacs, which had burst into violent bloom. All at once, the sweet fragrance reminded me of what Carola de Florent, my parents' friend and neighbor, wrote to me after their deaths: "Each had a specific and intense sweetness which I describe to myself as the essence of intelligence. I doubt that you will quite accept my word. No child could. There is too much exchange of power between parent and child for the term sweetness to fit comfortably." Yet now that their power is spent, I taste their sweetness.

Yes, it was fitting, I concluded, that the house they had exuberantly inhabited for forty years should be again, in Dad's final judgment of Mom, "so full of life." Suddenly fierce with my new reality, I clasped the doctor's hand with Dad's grip and held his eyes with Mom's gaze and, speaking for us all, wished his family the complicated pleasures of long life.

Baking Bread with My Daughter

KATHLEEN DEAN MOORE

In the cabin, my daughter kneaded bread. The dough was thick, un-
wieldy, and it took all her strength to turn it. When I looked at her, I
hardly recognized this woman-child, her face all planes and no softness. She reached across her body to rub her shoulder, leaving flour
on her shirt.

This pain has no logic. It makes no sense. There is nothing to be
learned from illness in a person so young. The only fact is pain, and
the wooden slab of a daughter's face.

"I don't think of it that way," she said. "You can't know in ad-
vance if something's good or bad." She turned the bread under her
hands and pushed against it with her fists. Fists on dough. A rough,
heavy dough: sesame seeds, wheat berries, rye seeds. It will make a
good, thick, nutritious bread. "I've seen people who can't tell the
difference between what hurts them and what helps them," she said,
"and I don't want to be like that." She turned the bread over on itself
and folded over the folding. The expanding dough resisted the turning, pulled away from her fists. The dough had ideas. She pushed it
against the side of the bowl. As she kneaded, her face began to relax.

"There is pain that hurts and pain that heals," she said, and I
knew she was right. Move even if it hurts, the doctor had told her.

With fibromyalgia, this is the way you get well. Healing takes time. Let it hurt, but gently.

Flour and yeast and water. She set the starter on the top shelf of the woodstove and put another log in the firebox. After a time, she added sugar and oil, and more flour, and then all the seeds in the bag. The more she pushed on the dough, folded it over, pressed it with the heels of her hands, the more it rebounded. It's hard for a mother, you know, to see a child bear up. I cried in the kitchen, and then I was ashamed. "What's wrong?" she asked, but the pain in me was the pain in her and she divided the dough into two pieces and shaped it into two loaves.

"What I need from you," she said, "is for you to sprinkle corn-meal on the baking pan." So I did. She took a round loaf in two hands and laid it gently on the pan. Then the other.

The loaves are on the shelf under a tea towel. She can't put them in the oven yet, because we've got the stove too hot. It would harden the loaves before they finish rising. So gently now. Not too much heat. I am trying to learn this. Believe me, I am trying. There will be time for more logs in the firebox. There will be time for an oven heated to 400 degrees. We come away and let it rest. Sometimes patience is as good as hope.

Two egg whites, beaten. Brush them on the risen loaves. Out the kitchen window, there is wind in the birches. Little curls of bark tear away from the trunks and scatter across the patchy snow. The new bark underneath is pure white. Poppy seeds sprinkled on round loaves. Round loaves in the oven, hardening around the edges, still rising in the center. The crust cracks, and steam puffs out the fissures.

Only a few days ago, the birches were noisy with yellow leaves, shuffling in the wind. When we heard leaves blowing across the road, we thought a car was coming; they were that loud. But now the leaves have twisted off the trees and blown onto the lake.

There are fishermen on the bay in their silver boats, leaning over their poles, their hands clasped between their knees; and bear hunters past the portages. We saw them pass today, canoes heavy with gear.

The radio says a cold Arctic air mass is headed into northern Minnesota. There is no color in the sun. Soon we will wake up to a new calm. The lake will be white and shining, with birch leaves frozen in the surface. In heavy coats, my daughter and I will walk on the lake. What will we have learned about winter? What will we know about stillness that we didn't know before?

Viriditas *in Vinci*

JUDITH SORNBERGER

In the middle of the journey of my life, I went searching for the Virgin in the museums and churches of Tuscany. Vinci hadn't appeared on the list of sites my friend Martha and I had planned to visit. But toward the end of our trip, as we prepared to leave San Gimignano, we perused the map for a place of interest that wouldn't be too far out of the way as we returned to Florence. By this point in the trip we were looking for someplace simple to locate and to see in just one day.

Finding the village was a snap. From there we drove into the countryside fragrant with olive trees to find the hilltop farmhouse where Leonardo da Vinci was born. Doves swooped and bees moaned along on their ancient errands as we climbed the hill from our car to his patio.

Inside the modest stone house, the air was cool, dark, and damp. No efforts had been made to "museumize" the place. No period furniture, carpets, books, or crockery were arranged to make it seem as though the seventeen-year-old Leonardo might have left the house just that morning to travel to Florence for his apprenticeship in the studio of Verrocchio. Probably most shocking of all was the lack of art on the walls. What had I expected—a few Simone Martinis scattered around, a fresco or two by Fra Angelico?

I knew that Leonardo was the acknowledged illegitimate son of a Vinci lawyer who underwrote his art training. But what of his life here in this cottage? What was his mother like? Did she have the soul of an artist? Maybe his aesthetic sense developed as he watched her arranging flowers from the garden outside for the table. I wondered if she sat on the stone patio with him some afternoons watching the bees and the doves. Might her sense of wonder have infected him?

When I tried to see him here in her care, my imagination kept hitting stone walls, the same way it did whenever I wanted to know more about Mary than the Bible revealed. As the mother of sons, I wanted to reach behind the legends surrounding Leonardo and yank out her story—how she came to live in this house, to give birth to this more-or-less fatherless son, to raise such an inquisitive child. How did she support herself and her son, or did Leonardo's father cover their living expenses? The guidebooks were mute on these issues, implying by their silence that he had sprung fully formed from his father's purse at age seventeen. But since I had been a single mother myself for several years following my divorce from the boys' father and had struggled to put cereal and beanie-wienies on the table, these were important questions to me.

At least we know Mary's name and how she came to give birth to a son who also would have been deemed illegitimate. And there are some parts of the story—the Annunciation, the Visitation, the Nativity—in which she takes center stage. But after visiting Leonardo's home, I understood more than ever the impulse that had created the apocryphal stories of Mary's own conception, nativity, and childhood. Unfortunately, her story goes underground once Jesus is launched on his mission and doesn't reemerge until after his execution. There has been endless speculation about how Jesus spent his years as a young man before his ministry began. Of course, I'm curious about that, too. But, even more, I want to know how Mary spent those years—and the years when he was on the road. I want to know what she was pondering in her heart, to know her as a woman, not only as an icon.

Maybe that's why I love the story of the marriage at Cana and the hints it offers about the dynamic between mother and son. Mary says, *Look, son, they're out of wine. Why don't you help them out?* And Jesus answers, *Forget it, Mom. I'm not supposed to be performing any miracles yet.* At which point she gives him (I like to think) *the look,* and he changes the water to wine like a good boy. I know that this first miracle is supposed to demonstrate Jesus' respect for marriage and to foreshadow the wine of the Last Supper. But I think it shows that Mary helped her son develop his sense of responsibility for his gifts and the way he used them. And that she was not overawed by his birthright or abilities. Finally, I think it reveals that Jesus still knew better than to disobey his mother.

By the time we reach the end of their story, Mary's son has traveled infinitely beyond her ability to care for—or even counsel— him. At the cloister of San Marco in Florence, Fra Angelico had painted a fresco for each of the monks' cells, each one a moment from the Gospels, so that walking the corridors was like taking a small journey through Christ's life. I had delighted in the jewel tones of the Annunciation, the Nativity, and the Transfiguration, but felt my footsteps quickening as I passed the cells that held the later, darker scenes of the story. I had been horrified to find that one entire corridor was filled with frescoes of the Crucifixion, especially when I discovered that these were the novices' cells. How would it be to sleep under that agony each night, the blood so bright even now that it must have looked about to drop onto their pillows? I felt especially sorry for those young sleepers from hundreds of years ago when I considered that many of them were newly arrived from the comforts of their mothers' goodnight kisses.

I thought again of Mary. What nightmare could be more un-
bearable for a mother than the one revealed in those frescoes—a
woman witnessing her child's pain, helpless to do anything to end it?
And what image could be more universal, at least for mothers, for
don't we all at some point have to stand by and watch our offspring
suffering?

The fresco that I couldn't hurry past was Angelico's *Christ Res-
urrected*. It should be a joyous painting, for the angel taps Mary's
shoulder and points upward to a gleaming bubble in which the risen
Christ is floating. But Mary pays the angel no attention. Seated on
the edge of the sarcophagus, she leans into the tomb below, shading
her eyes from the glare above, searching for the body she gave birth
to. Eventually, she will hear the angel's message and maybe even rejoice. But right now she needs to stare into the darkness, into the
depths of her loss. And I needed for a while to stand there with her.

⁓

Even as a modern woman living in an era that is fairly ho-hum
about rocket ships, computers, and even cloning, I was amazed by
what I found in the Museo Leonardiano in a restored thirteenth-
century castle in downtown Vinci. Alongside drawings from his
notebooks were dozens of full-scale models built of pine, including
a bicycle, a flying machine, and a diver's breathing apparatus. I
had known that Leonardo had studied anatomy, mathematics, and
philosophy as well as art and that he had dreamed up devices that
were several centuries before their time. But to see them laid out in
a smorgasbord that ran the gamut from domestic conveniences,
such as a vacuum cleaner, to military weapons, running from the
brilliant to the absurd, was awe-inspiring. His inventions demon-
strated his genius, of course, but even more compelling to me was
the way they revealed the voraciousness of his intellect and his soul's
drive to create.

That lushness of spirit must have been what the twelfth-century German abbess Hildegard Von Bingen had had in mind when she coined the term *viriditas*—literally "greening power"—to refer to the force that drove, and continues to drive, creation. The epitome of a Renaissance woman three hundred years before the Renaissance began, Hildegard herself was a walking, talking model of *viriditas*. A visionary, writer, herbalist, skilled healer, and savvy politician, Hildegard is best known to us today for the wildly original, polyphonic sacred music she composed for her nuns to sing in the convent she founded in Rupertsberg on the Rhine. And for the female-based theology revealed in her lyrics. In one antiphon to Mary, she argues that, although a woman (Eve) had opened the door to death for human beings, another woman had "subdued" death. Therefore, she posits, women are the highest form of life. Now there's invention for you—taking the story of woman that has been used to denigrate and oppress women and turning it on its head so that she comes out the hero of the tale! You've got to love her audacity.

~

The night following our day in Vinci I dreamed that my son Jamie was giving me a ride on the handlebars of his bike the way, as children, my friends and I would sometimes ride. I remarked on the fact that now he was the one carrying me, whereas, when he was little, I had pedaled the bike as he sat in the child's seat behind me. Riding through a tunnel, we came upon his brother, Matt, sitting on the ground writing something. As we drew closer, we could see that it was some kind of angry diatribe against his boss—a woman. But I was staring at the handwriting itself, which was intricate calligraphy. Despite his indignation, he couldn't seem to keep himself from making something beautiful of it. "Matt, you could be an artist," I whispered, amazed. "Remember, you always were artistic, even as a kid."

The bike was an obvious reference to the bicycle Leonardo had designed. But I think it also referred to the cycles of our lives. When Jamie was just out of babyhood, a glass had broken on our kitchen floor and his cornea had been injured. The astigmatism resulting from the corrective surgery had caused the eye to turn in, making him a target for cruelty at school. Even worse had been the developmental and learning problems that followed. I was extremely protective of him. Even after he was a young adult I had swooped in to rescue him, probably inappropriately, on numerous occasions. But in the dream he was the powerful one, capable not only of getting himself where he needed to go, but also of giving me a ride, since I seemed to recall that he was taking me to buy an airline ticket (a nod to Leonardo's flying machine?).

My other son, Matt, had struggled with anger since adolescence. I had always wondered if there was some grievous flaw in my mothering that had dug him into a trough of brooding resentment that he could never rise from for very long, despite his charming winsomeness. Once, not long after my divorce from the boys' father, I had stopped at the elementary school to pick them up, but they were nowhere to be seen. I panicked immediately, certain that some maniac had lured them into his car with the promise of some toy I couldn't afford. I prowled the surrounding blocks, asking every boy on the street if he had seen them. Finally, one boy pointed toward a wooded area behind the school grounds. I parked and ran over there, my heart pounding with the fear of what I would find.

Within a circle of pines stood a circle of boys, including Jamie. Inside stood Matt and another boy, squaring off to fight. I didn't want to completely humiliate him, so I stood there until he noticed me. I crooked my finger at him, and he started toward me, glowering. Jamie came, too, looking a little pleased that his brother might be in trouble, and the other boys broke into twos and threes, heading off in different directions. Matt never said what the impending fight was all about.

Once I got over my relief, though, I started worrying about the other kinds of damage my sons had suffered—not at some stranger's hands but at the hands of the people charged with their care. I recalled the night when I was tucking the boys in and Matt had said, "Dad told us we could all be together again if it was all right with you." How stubborn and arbitrary I must have seemed to him as I tried to tell him, without really telling him, why that couldn't happen. In the years to come he became more silent, harder to read or to reach. In the dream he was still entrenched in anger, yet I could see his potential for artistry, for creating his own life without my worry or "help."

The dream suggested that I was finally ready to let my sons propel themselves and discover their true gifts, that I was learning to see them as the geniuses of their own lives. Maybe "posthumous therapist" could be added to Leonardo's long list of accomplishments.

What both Jesus' and Leonardo's mothers—and Hildegard's mother, too, who sent her daughter off to the nunnery at age eight—did best for their gifted progeny was allow them to go their own ways. Doing so, it seems to me, requires immense faith. Not a simplistic belief that everything will turn out for the best in the end, but a faith that one's child will invent a life that is not necessarily safe but that is rich and passionate.

It is the same kind of faith that creation requires. For in order to create one must be willing to be a fool—to fail, to look ridiculous. One must sense the energy of the thing to be created and give oneself over to participating in its making. One must lose control. Not every song or painting or invention is beautiful or brilliant. How well I know it! And as a writer I take heart from the fact that the same Leonardo who discovered the true source of fossils also drew something as ludicrous as the fellow in court dress balancing on water, his feet fastened to inflated skins, his hands holding some kind of ski poles. And I love that he wanted to make it possible for us to do what only Jesus had done. Certainly, his faith outshone Peter's.

What I cherish, admire, and delight in about the Hildegards and Leonardos of our world is not the way they tower over the rest of us mere mortals in their great genius. Rather, it is that they seek to bridge the gap between this world and the one beyond our senses *via the senses*. Hildegard dictated her visions to her faithful secretary, who both transcribed them and painted them so that we could see what she saw when she was seized by the Divine. She created her haunting songs so that we could hear what angels sounded like—indeed, so that we could, through singing her music, become angels. In each of his sketches, Leonardo, too, pushes us beyond the known, beyond the expected, beyond our dreams of what is possible.

If Hildegard was right, the same generative force that powers all green and breathing things pulses through each of us and is the source of all we make as well. In one song she addresses Mary as *"viridissima virga"*—greenest branch. On this trip to Tuscany an unexpected call toward faith had echoed from the marble walls of abbeys, from frescoes, and church bell towers, one that felt as irresistible as the call to greenness that each branch must feel as winter recedes. A call to faith in the God I had rejected for more than twenty years, certainly. But also faith in my mothering—despite its inevitable flaws—the tree from which my sons now traveled in their own green directions.

———

Let's say it is the first gentle spring afternoon, and a young woman sits on the stone wall surrounding her patio, a basket of needlework at her feet. Her young son has asked her for the use of a needle and thread, which she gives him without asking how he plans to use it. She is used to his wanting to surprise her with sketches of bees and moths and birds. As she stitches she casts bemused glances at his back turned to prevent her spying his latest endeavor.

Let's say that on this day, rather than drawing in his notebook, the boy is tearing precious blank sheets from it. But his mother hums a soft tune and pretends to hear nothing. He stays bent over his work on the stone patio after she has gone inside to begin their dinner. She sings as she chops and stirs. Her song drifts through the unshuttered window, and he stitches to the rhythm of her song. When she comes to the door to call him in, she doesn't see him. Leonardo, *she calls, pretending to be frightened at his disappearance.* My son, where are you? *From around the corner of their cottage a boy-sized bird swoops through twilight's curtain, its white paper wings catching the moonlight.*

Let's say she claps her hands. Let's say she calls it good.

Scars: In Four Parts

SALLIE TISDALE

1982—wound (woond) n. [OE. wund] an injury in which the skin or other tissue is broken, cut, torn, etc.

Four years ago he was born and everything changed. Daily we leave jobs, friends, lovers, but the child always comes along. When the going gets rough, my son and I can't call it quits and cut our losses. I can't pack a bag, make a break for it, find a more compatible child. The contract cannot be broken.

We are strangely entangled. When I wake from a bad dream without a sound, he wakes in the next room and cries for me. Between us there is no shame, no holding back. I take risks with him I wouldn't dare take with anyone else. I treat him with rough impatience, with all the bile I hide from friends and lovers for fear of losing them. I am less tolerant of deviation, more injured by separation. We fight, and then make up with a tentative, weary kiss. I demand so much: loyalty, obedience, faith. And he gives me all I demand, and more—he thinks me beautiful; he wants to grow up to be just like me. And I am bound to fail him, and bound to lose him. Strangers' hands will stroke where I stroke now, and already I'm jealous of this secret future apart from me.

I quail at the mistakes I'm bound to make, what I'll saddle him with, what the price for each of us will finally be. For nothing is free. Daily the gap between us grows, in tiny steps. He is not mindful of it—but I am. Oh, I am. I'll give the world a son, heavy with the grief of giving him at all. Then and after, he'll drift in and out of my view, keeping secrets, neglecting me, while I watch from a distance, unrequited.

My mother shows up, startling me, when I speak to my son. I repeat what she told me, the phrases and platitudes, in the same tone of voice and inflection I heard as a child. She is my forebear; I am his inheritance, and will prevail despite his efforts. Years from now I'll show up, a sudden surprise.

Could my own mother have felt this fierce love for me? I treat her so casually. If she ever felt this way it seems she should be grieved—bereft by my distance. Can it be that she misses me? We don't speak of such things: our closest contacts are narrowly averted, sudden swerves from danger. Will it be the same for my son and me, the boy who now crawls like a spoiled child-prince across my lap?

"When I grow up," he tells me, "you'll be my baby."

1986—dehiscence (de-his´ens) [L. dihīscere, to gape] A bursting open, as of... a wound...

He's tall now, and lean: when he comes running toward me, breathless from some grand injustice or new idea, I see his ribs pressing against the skin, light and shadow. He takes deep, thoughtless breaths, free of blemish, taut and promising. He has my brother's face, a handsome face, and he wears his lucky muscles with negligence, and not a whit of gratitude. He is eight years old.

Sudden sufficiency. What binds us is less visible, as though we'd been cloven in two. I would not have thought it possible to feel so halved. I can wonder now what it is like to be him—wonder, and know I'll never know. What does he think in a privacy I can hardly bear, a privacy that seems entirely unfair? I am still the dictator of this tiny country; he is still my subject, but he dreams of revolution.

I may not kiss him in front of others anymore. He holds the car door for me, calls me "Ma'am," with a giggle. He has great white teeth, dark circles below his eyes, a scratch on his cheek, dirt in the lines of his neck. He wants his hair cut "like Elvis Presley," he wants it cut "like Michael Jackson," he wants a Mohawk. He sings commercial jingles for hamburgers and jeans and toothpaste while he builds elaborate block constructions; he strews his room with Viewmasters and action figures ("They're not *dolls*, Mom," he says in irritation) and books and dirty socks and sheets. He is, above all, busy; I am tired. "You are," he tells me, "more beautiful than the women in *Playboy*," and he's out the door before I can ask where he saw *Playboy*.

How does he know the exact inflection? He has the same disgust and injured dignity I felt all those years ago, dying a thousand deaths in the face of my mother's twittering concerns. He comes into his own and it is my turn to be out-of-date, to be shocked, to drone on long after he ceases to hear me. I am, he tells me, so *old*.

The neighbor boys tease him and he runs home in a paroxysm of despair. "No one likes me," he sobs, and lends to his crying a thorough attention. What courage children have. I lead him to the dentist and he climbs shakily in the great chair, looks at me, and asks me to spare him this. I won't; seeing my refusal, he turns away. He wants me to keep him a baby, he doesn't know that I would if I could. Already *I* am separate. He looks at me and sees—only me.

He is an infant again, arms around my thighs, moaning with

love, whining for cereal, a story, my lap. But he's too lanky, too long, for my lap; his elbows get in the way of the book. Then he looks for the mysterious pleasures of adulthood: freedom, mobility, explanations. But his brow furrows when he calculates the cost.

At night he is drenched in protest. He licks his teeth clean, stumbles out of the bathroom in a dirty T-shirt and yesterday's underwear, crawls over the mess on the floor of his room, and hides his stuffed bunny shamefully under the covers. I wait. And when he falls into the humid sleep of children, that greenhouse dark, I slip stealthily in beside him and stroke his honey hair. He sprawls out, clutching the bunny; I balance on the edge, listening to the ruffled quiver of his breaths. I stroke the fear, my fear, of his life, his death. When I contemplate the space he takes up, how vast its emptiness would be, my heart shakes like a rabbit in the jaws of the wolf. I watch his face turned soft with sleep, the smile that skips across his face as he turns snug and safe, and I can see that he's dreaming. He dreams without me now; we dream different dreams.

The balance is shifting. I withdraw sometimes; I want to read my book or be alone when he craves my attention. He will always live with me, he says, or perhaps next door. A transparent gift of beauty is evolving in his bones and skin, beauty made of equal parts grace and pain; I see that he will have a face of triumphant perfection if he wants. And I see the bruises rising under his skin from life's blows. I know he won't live next door, and I'm glad. I don't think I can bear to watch. Right now, I can't remember life without him—I can't remember *myself* without him, but the time will come.

I put my book aside and wander to his room to watch him play. I find him reading a book, curled in a corner.

"Would you mind leaving, Mom?" he says, hardly glancing up. "I feel like being alone."

**1993—inflammation (in′fle-mā′shen) [<l. inflammation
—*see* inflame]** redness, swelling, pain, tenderness, heat

I wait in the car in the grocery store parking lot, watching the
bright automatic doors in my rearview mirror. It is almost ten
o'clock at night, much later than usual for me to be out shopping. For
fifteen years I've been confined to childish hours. But everything
changes.

I see him walk out the middle set of doors, which slide silently
apart and then close behind him. He is tall, several inches taller than
me, slender, graceful, arrogant. He wears his thick hair in a high
tuft, dyed boot-black, and his black leather silver-studded jacket
swings open with each long step.

I used to have crushes on boys like him.

We all have blows—we learn to expect a few, to roll in the force
of life's fist. That awful job, that last paycheck, the broken heart, the
broken nose. All the broken promises no one has even made yet—
wounds that can't be helped. I don't have to fear failing him anymore—I already have. What's done is done.

But I hadn't expected this.

I hadn't expected to be knocked to my knees in grief when he
marches out after I tell him to stay, when he slams the door and disappears, and I drive through dark streets seeking him, and find him
smoking in the park with the silent, leggy girlfriend who won't speak
to me at all. I draw myself up, demand *decency, respect;* they stare, and
whisper to each other.

And I hadn't expected the sorry business of petty crime. He's
been arrested for shoplifting—for stealing candy bars, for stealing
cigarettes, for stealing condoms. I drive to juvenile hall again and
face the disapproving eyes behind bulletproof glass, and sign the
papers, and wait outside until I'm joined by a raggedy, rude, foul-

mouthed boy I hardly know. We drive home in silence and as we walk in the door I tell him to wash the dishes and he says, "No," and I say it again and he refuses again and then adds, mockingly, "And I don't want to have to say it again." And suddenly I'm soaked with white rage, a face-slapping high-dive, and I'm inches from his face, brandishing the nearest object, yelling, Don't you dare, don't you dare, don't you *dare* speak to me that way.

When we're calm, I can see he thinks I miss the point, the urgent momentum of growing up. I seem to have no ground, nothing to rely upon. He calls me a "disagreeable old hag" at the dinner table and suddenly it makes me laugh. It's so absurd. I saw my parents' anguish in my own small crimes from a cool distance; I remember their stupefaction. I drew up painful words for them deliberately, like poison into a syringe. Children grow into strangers who disappoint and perplex us, having long wakened to disillusionment with us. They seem oblivious to our loss—after all, they've lost nothing. We are their parents. And now it's my turn and I am so sorry now for what I did then.

He disappears for three days and I cannot find him. The fear is horrible, sickening; the remorse and guilt meaningless, confused. Then his girlfriend's mother calls me to tell me he's staying there because we "kicked him out," and I try to tell her it's not true, to send him home so he will work it out with me, and she refuses. She believes him, his tales. I ask her not to shelter him from this. "I'm going to take care of him," she tells me. "*I* like him."

When he finally returns, we fight round after round, and there's no bell. Every victory is a Pyrrhic victory. *Baby*, I want to say, *baby love, I don't know what to do. Show me what to do.* Harsh words again, the stomp of heavy boots up the stairs. From two floors above me he lets loose a deep-throated cry, an animal cry, and then the noise of something heavy thrown with what seems an irrevocable, rending crash.

1997—scar (skär) [<MFr.<LL. <Gr. *eschara*, orig. hearth]
a mark left after a wound, burn, ulcer, etc. has healed

Like all the other scars, this one is slowly filling in, closing off. Scars may be tender, or numb, but they are always there. Scars change the shape of things—they wrinkle, tighten, shorten things. I brought this person into the world and everything turned upside-down, and all that's happened since has been in some way connected to that event, his birth. The parent-child bond, I know, is truly bondage, and its end is in many ways a liberation, an enormous relief. Here he comes, hat in hand, to claim himself and go.

He is nineteen, towering above me, his voice booming on the telephone. He is gorgeous. He is not a virgin; he admits that he is in love. He is kind to his little sister, worries about his carefree older brother. Every day, changes: he drops out of high school, grabs a quick diploma at the community college, makes plans, finds a job, is shockingly responsible. He gets a checking account and an 800 number and big ideas: conspiracy theories and politics, tales of hidden alien artifacts and government cabals. His union goes on strike and he walks the picket line with all the other working men. He is righteous, indignant, a defender of the weak, and I bite my lip not to laugh and cry at once; oh god, it's the way I was at nineteen, it's exactly the way I was.

He absents himself delicately from my life.

One day he stops me in the hall, without warning, dragging his foot and looking at the floor, and mumbles, "I'm sorry," and I ask him for what and he says, "Because I was so hard," and without meeting my eyes he reaches down from his height to hug me awkwardly and adds, "I love you, Mom" and dashes down the stairs and is gone, again.

from

The Cancer Journals

AUDRE LORDE

Each woman responds to the crisis that breast cancer brings to her life out of a whole pattern, which is the design of who she is and how her life has been lived. The weave of her everyday existence is the training ground for how she handles crisis. Some women obscure their painful feelings surrounding mastectomy with a blanket of business-as-usual, thus keeping those feelings forever under cover, but expressed elsewhere. For some women, in a valiant effort not to be seen as merely victims, this means an insistence that no such feelings exist and that nothing much has occurred. For some women it means the warrior's painstaking examination of yet another weapon, unwanted but useful.

I am a postmastectomy woman who believes our feelings need voice in order to be recognized, respected, and of use.

I do not wish my anger and pain and fear about cancer to fossilize into yet another silence, nor to rob me of whatever strength can lie at the core of this experience, openly acknowledged and examined. For other women of all ages, colors, and sexual identities who recognize that imposed silence about any area of our lives is a tool for separation and powerlessness, and for myself, I have tried to voice some of my feelings and thoughts about the travesty of prosthesis, the pain of amputation, the function of cancer in a profit economy, my confrontation with mortality, the strength of women loving, and the power and rewards of self-conscious living.

Breast cancer and mastectomy are not unique experiences, but ones shared by thousands of American women. Each of these women has a particular voice to be raised in what must become a female outcry against all preventable cancers, as well as against the secret fears that allow those cancers to flourish. May these words serve as encouragement for other women to speak and to act out of our experiences with cancer and with other threats of death, for silence has never brought us anything of worth. Most of all, may these words underline the possibilities of self-healing and the richness of living for all women.

There is a commonality of isolation and painful reassessment which is shared by all women with breast cancer, whether this commonality is recognized or not. It is not my intention to judge the woman who has chosen the path of prosthesis, of silence and invisibility, the woman who wishes to be "the same as before." She has survived on another kind of courage, and she is not alone. Each of us struggles daily with the pressures of conformity and the loneliness of difference from which those choices seem to offer escape. I only know that those choices do not work for me, nor for other women who, not without fear, have survived cancer by scrutinizing its meaning within our lives, and by attempting to integrate this crisis into useful strengths for change.

⁓

These selected journal entries . . . begin 6 months after my modified radical mastectomy for breast cancer; [they] exemplify the process of integrating this crisis into my life.

1.26.79

I'm not feeling very hopeful these days, about selfhood or anything else. I handle the outward motions of each day while pain fills me like a puspocket and every touch threatens to breech the taut membrane that keeps it from flowing through and poisoning my whole existence. Sometimes despair sweeps across my consciousness like lunar winds across a barren moonscape. Ironshod horses rage back and forth over every nerve. Oh Seboulisa ma, help me remember what I have paid so much to learn. I could die of difference, or live—myriad selves.

2.5.79

The terrible thing is that nothing goes past me these days, nothing. Each horror remains like a steel vise in my flesh, another magnet to the flame. Buster has joined the rolecall of useless wasteful deaths of young Black people; in the gallery today everywhere ugly images of women offering up distorted bodies for whatever fantasy passes in the name of male art. Gargoyles of pleasure. Beautiful laughing Buster, shot down in a hallway for ninety cents. Shall I unlearn that tongue in which my curse is written?

3.1.79

It is such an effort to find decent food in this place, not to just give up and eat the old poison. But I must tend my body with at least as much care as I tend the compost, particularly now when it seems so beside the point. Is this pain and despair that surround me a result of cancer, or has it just been released by cancer? I feel so unequal to what I always handled before, the abominations outside that echo the pain within. And yes I am

completely self-referenced right now because it is the only translation I can trust, and I do believe not until every woman traces
her weave back strand by bloody self referenced strand, will we
begin to alter the whole pattern.

4.16.79

The enormity of our task, to turn the world around. It feels like
turning my life around, inside out. If I can look directly at my life
and my death without flinching I know there is nothing they can
ever do to me again. I must be content to see how really little I
can do and still do it with an open heart. Last spring was another
piece of the fall and winter before, a progression from all the
pain and sadness of that time, ruminated over. But somehow this
summer which is almost upon me feels like a part of my future.
Like a brand new time, and I'm pleased to know it, wherever it
leads. I feel like another woman, de-chrysalised and become a
broader, stretched-out me, strong and excited, a muscle flexed
and honed for action.

6.20.80

I do not forget cancer for very long, ever. That keeps me armed
and on my toes, but also with a slight background noise of fear.
Carl Simonton's book, *Getting Well Again,* has been really helpful
to me, even though his smugness infuriates me sometimes. The
visualizations and deep relaxing techniques that I learned from
it help make me a less anxious person, which seems strange, because in other ways, I live with the constant fear of recurrence of
another cancer. But fear and anxiety are not the same at all. One
is an appropriate response to a real situation which I can accept
and learn to work through just as I work through semiblindness.

But the other, anxiety, is an immobilizing yield to things that go bump in the night, a surrender to namelessness, formlessness, voicelessness, and silence.

7.10.80

I dreamt I had begun training to change my life, with a teacher who is very shadowy. I was not attending classes, but I was going to learn how to change my whole life, live differently, do everything in a new and different way. I didn't really understand, but I trusted this shadowy teacher. Another young woman who was there told me she was taking a course in "language crazure," the opposite of discrazure (the cracking and wearing away of rock). I thought it would be very exciting to study the formation and crack and composure of words, so I told my teacher I wanted to take that course. My teacher said okay, but it wasn't going to help me any because I had to learn something else, and I wouldn't get anything new from that class. I replied maybe not, but even though I knew all about rocks, for instance, I still liked studying their composition, and giving a name to the different ingredients of which they were made. It's very exciting to think of me being all the people in this dream.

I have learned much in the 18 months since my mastectomy. My visions of a future I can create have been honed by the lessons of my limitations. Now I wish to give form with honesty and precision to the pain faith labor and loving which this period of my life has translated into strength for me.

Sometimes fear stalks me like another malignancy, sapping energy and power and attention from my work. A cold becomes sinister; a cough, lung cancer; a bruise, leukemia. Those fears are most powerful when they are not given voice, and close upon their heels comes the fury that I cannot shake them. I am learning to live beyond fear by living through it, and in the process learning to turn fury at my own limitations into some more creative energy. I realize that if I wait until I am no longer afraid to act, write, speak, be, I'll be sending messages on a ouija board, cryptic complaints from the other side. When I dare to be powerful, to use my strength in the service of my vision, then it becomes less important whether or not I am unafraid.

As women we were raised to fear. If I cannot banish fear completely, I can learn to count with it less. For then fear becomes not a tyrant against which I waste my energy fighting, but a companion, not particularly desirable, yet one whose knowledge can be useful.

I write so much here about fear because in shaping this introduction to *The Cancer Journals*, I found fear laid across my hands like a steel bar. When I tried to reexamine the 18 months since my mastectomy, some of what I touched was molten despair and waves of mourning—for my lost breast, for time, for the luxury of false power. Not only were these emotions difficult and painful to relive, but they were entwined with the terror that if I opened myself once again to scrutiny, to feeling the pain of loss, of despair, of victories too minor in my eyes to rejoice over, then I might also open myself again to disease. I had to remind myself that I had lived through it all, already. I had known the pain, and survived it. It only remained for me to give it voice, to share it for use, that the pain not be wasted.

Living a self-conscious life, under the pressure of time, I work with the consciousness of death at my shoulder, not constantly, but often enough to leave a mark upon all of my life's decisions and actions. And it does not matter whether this death comes next week or thirty years from now; this consciousness gives my life another breadth. It helps shape the words I speak, the ways I love, my politic of action, the strength of my vision and purpose, the depth of my appreciation of living.

I would lie if I did not also speak of loss. Any amputation is a physical and psychic reality that must be integrated into a new sense of self. The absence of my breast is a recurrent sadness, but certainly not one that dominates my life. I miss it, sometimes piercingly. When other one-breasted women hide behind the mask of prosthesis or the dangerous fantasy of reconstruction, I find little support in the broader female environment for my rejection of what feels like a cosmetic sham. But I believe that socially sanctioned prosthesis is merely another way of keeping women with breast cancer silent and separate from each other. For instance, what would happen if an army of one-breasted women descended upon Congress and demanded that the use of carcinogenic, fat-stored hormones in beef-feed be outlawed?

The lessons of the past 18 months have been many: How do I provide myself with the best physical and psychic nourishment to repair past, and minimize future damage to my body? How do I give voice to my quests so that other women can take what they need from my experiences? How do my experiences with cancer fit into the larger tapestry of my work as a Black woman, into the history of all women? And most of all, how do I fight the despair born of fear and anger and powerlessness which is my greatest internal enemy?

I have found that battling despair does not mean closing my eyes to the enormity of the tasks of effecting change, nor ignoring the strength and the barbarity of the forces aligned against us. It means teaching, surviving and fighting with the most important resource I have, myself, and taking joy in that battle. It means, for me, recognizing the enemy outside and the enemy within, and knowing that my work is part of a continuum of women's work, of reclaiming this earth and our power, and knowing that this work did not begin with my birth nor will it end with my death. And it means knowing that within this continuum, my life and my love and my work has particular power and meaning relative to others.

It means trout fishing on the Missisquoi River at dawn and tasting the green silence, and knowing that this beauty too is mine forever.

29 August 1980

Saying Yes, Yes, Always Yes

SANDY BOUCHER

The heart is always the place to go. Go home into your heart, where there is warmth, appreciation, gratitude and contentment.

AYYA KHEMA

It is now eight years since I was diagnosed with colon cancer. Periodically I have a colonoscopy, which so far shows no tumor or other growth in my intestines. If there are cancer cells lurking in my body, they have attacked no organs yet, for which I am grateful. I find myself grateful for many things just now, particularly the writing of my memoir, *Hidden Spring*, which required me to return to and re-live the most painful year of my life, a process that was sometimes excruciating.

Why did I choose to write of that experience? There had been a moment, during one of my hospitalizations, that persuaded me to do so. That day the head surgeon visited me. His name was Dr. Organ (no kidding) and he was a large, brown-skinned, handsome man who radiated the kind of confidence that comes from substantial accomplishment and recognition. Dr. Organ was interested in my being a writer, and we discussed the books on the table next to my bed. As I explained to him what each was about, I felt a little embarrassed: would he think I was morbid in my literary tastes, given my condition? Yet Dr. Organ listened with great interest.

When he left the room and I was alone again, I looked at the books I had brought with me to the hospital. *Diary of a Zen Nun*, luminously written, explored, among other things, the author Nan Shin's experience of ovarian cancer; Isabel Allende chronicled the slow dying of her daughter in *Paula;* Audre Lorde, African American lesbian poet-warrior, in *A Burst of Light,* wrote of her struggle with liver cancer. A visiting friend, seeing this small angst-ridden library, had asked me, "Why would you want to read *this* stuff!?"

The answer was that I could stomach nothing but this vision that looked straight at death. I wanted to hear from those who had gone where I found myself, and farther. I wanted to hear what thoughts they had, what they felt, whether they could meet their suffering bravely or if they crumpled before it, and if there was meaning in it for them. In Dr. Organ's wake, lifting these books and holding them, I thought: If I have this need, others must feel it too. And I realized that I would write about my encounter with cancer, drawing another tiny map of the territory, to help the next woman or man who had to make this journey. As if to say, this is just how it is, someone else has walked this way.

During the writing of *Hidden Spring,* besides the necessary revisiting of pain and loss, I began to view my spiritual practice in a way that I never had before. In the months of producing the book I observed myself, sometimes with surprise, actually living my awareness with greater understanding than before.

The capacity to tolerate grief, loneliness, frustration, anger—to see those conditions as mind-states that will pass—is developing in me. Returning into the cancer time, I saw myself experiencing the truth that even in the midst of intense suffering, life bubbles up, offering joy. I saw how quickly our feelings and ideas about things pass: for this hour I am despairing, then suddenly delight comes, now I'm anxious, now confident. These mental states follow one upon the other endlessly. I saw that I watched them, participated in them, now and then wallowed in them, and let them go. Life continues to create itself and fall away, and suffering returns, and delight arrives, even for a moment—agony—peace—rapture. I learned not to imagine that any of these states will endure for very long. I did my best to tune in to the flow of phenomena, in which we are always in transit, bodies changing, emotions passing through a rainbow of feelings and thoughts; in which we are always inhabiting concepts and letting them go. I saw myself in the cancer months staying present to that flux.

Pema Chodron, in an early conversation about monasticism, said something that struck me. Monasticism removes so many of the props to our ego. Hair shorn; individuality hidden under the brown robe; focus sharpened by the schedule of meditation, study, and work, a truly practicing nun or monk gets herself or himself out of the way. And then what is experienced? Beaming at me, Pema described the immense creativity expressed in the arising and falling away of phenomena in every moment. I got the impression that her perception of this was like watching a brilliantly rich and entertaining performance.

While I am nowhere near that condition of clarity and detachment, I have come to more gratitude for the amount of reality that I *am* able to be aware of.

After I quit the chemo, four years ago, gradually over the ensuing weeks and months my body recovered from the assault of the poisons. I worked at getting well, building strength, hoping my damaged tissues would repair themselves. But I find that some of the effects of the chemotherapy still remain with me. I have almost no sense of smell, and my ability to taste has been diminished. I assume these changes are permanent, and I miss my former keen capacity to enjoy odors and tastes.

There is a deeper change. My identification with my body is seriously compromised. I have known its malfunction, its weakness; I have come close to losing this body to death. I had had experience in meditation of the impermanence of my physical self, its existence as flux, as a dance of energy. But now I sometimes perceive myself in quite ordinary social situations not as a solid entity but as a sheet of light passing through, or as unfocused vibration hovering in the scene.

In my spiritual practice, I plod slowly along on the road to bare attention, or "choiceless awareness." But I like to listen to a song by Heng Yin, an American-born Buddhist nun. Called "Great Is the Joy," the song evokes her feelings about the practice. One line says, "The sea of suffering is deep and wide [but] a turn of the head is the other side." That always reminds me that liberation is with us *now*, that with one sideways glance one may find oneself transported across the waters to the "other shore" of freedom from suffering.

Certainly joy is available to me in many ways. For the millennium I journeyed south to Dhamma Dena, to come home into the Dharma-stream sustained by my teacher, Ruth Denison. She was her usual indomitable self, even though her husband, Henry Denison, was experiencing the last process of his dying in a house not far from the meditation hall. Henry was attended by Dharma students and by Ruth herself whenever she could take time from the retreat to visit him. For forty years a strong bond had held them together: Henry was the person who had taken Ruth to Burma and introduced her to her teacher, U Ba Khin; she would always be loyal to him in gratitude for that priceless gift.

On December 31, 1999, the meditation hall was full of people who had come to escape the millennium/Y2K hysteria, to experience a sane, peaceful transition into the new year. We had rested an hour or two after the evening meal, put on our most festive-casual clothes, and arrived at the zendo to find our pillows arranged in a circle so that we could see each other. To begin, Ruth led the *Namo tassa* chant to the Buddha, and then she asked me to introduce a prayer and meditation we would share with people in every part of the globe. The notice I had received about this global prayer and meditation had projected that for New Year's Eve 2000 more than a billion people from all over the world would engage in a few moments of prayer or meditation for world peace. Once again we would acknowledge our interdependence with all life.

As our participation in this global effort, Ruth led a metta meditation, sending loving kindness to all beings in the universe. Then she asked us to stand up, and she improvised a dance. The night before, in her Dharma talk, she had explained the Eightfold Noble Path to enlightenment, dividing it into the usual three parts—*sila* (ethical conduct), *samadhi* (concentration), and *panna* (wisdom). Tonight she began to chant the three words, leading us in a sideways circle dance. *"Sila, Samadhi, Panna,"* we chanted as we sidestepped and dipped, and for some reason everyone seemed delighted. I felt the joy in movement, the meaning of the words. And I was so glad to be alive and to be here once again at Dhamma Dena. "Be mindful of your beautiful selves," Ruth reminded us. "Know what you are doing." And she swung out in a slow pirouette, lifting her hands as if inviting the celestial beings to join us.

After the dancing, Ruth sent us back to our pillows and brought out a large bag of used ribbons and gift wrappings. Approaching a rather dour, baldheaded man, she draped curled ribbons across his pate and taped them on to create a wacky holiday hat. Others rose to help her, and soon everyone was being decorated in more or less whimsical fashion. I found myself among the milliners, extracting bright paper from the bag, leaning over a seated meditator to shape yet another outrageous creation. And I realized that this willingness to participate so fully in an innocent and silly activity had developed in me after the cancer. Before, I might have sat locked in embarrassment or disapproval. But the cancer had pushed me fully into life.

As midnight approached, Ruth brought the big bell, shaped like a stew pot, to the center of the zendo. We would ring the bell 108 times, she announced. She would begin, and after ten strikes, someone else would take his or her turn. At the end of each ten strikes we were to call out some aspect of ourselves that we would like to get rid of. This is a traditional practice followed in the Zen tradition, based on the 36 delusions as they are perceived in the past, present, and future; the number can refer also to the 108 forms of enlightenment detailed in the Heart Sutra: one can imagine that as each negative quality is called out, a door to enlightenment is opened. Everyone gathered around the bell, and the ringing began.

While we counted together, I thought of my failures in the preceding year, most particularly my inability to relate evenly and compassionately with my partner. We had worked at repairing the relationship, and had experienced much forgiveness, but finally I had come to understand that I could never return into the partnership in a way that would be wholesome for both of us. I was not a *bodhisattva* motivated by endless compassion: I was a flawed person who had been wounded in a relationship and could not completely free myself from that legacy. With the ringing of the bell, I offered up my weakness, my selfishness and anger, and as each stroke fell into silence I vowed to strive to be more aware of my own behavior in the coming year, to open into more spaciousness. After the hundredth ring, Ruth took the striker and tolled the final eight tones to bring in the year 2000.

I looked around at the radiant faces of my Dharma-mates and

realized that we had entered the twenty-first century together, reinforcing the values of Buddha, Dharma, Sangha once again, committing ourselves to the path of liberation.

The evening ended with a meditation, led by Ruth, to renew our dedication to mindfulness of the body and to officially welcome the New Year.

I came out into the night, walked halfway between the meditation hall and the eating hall, and stood among the creosote and desert sage bushes, looking upward. The sky wheeled like a carousel above me, spinning arrows and dippers and great bright globes—all unexpectedly big and seeming very close. The sky dominated with its limitless depth, its fierce light, with very little competition from below—a few porch lights or window squares visible out across the flat black desert, Dhamma Dena's Christmas lights along the Zendo roof a feeble caterpillar glow. The stars seemed to strut and sail about, advertising their transcendence. It's no wonder the ancients made up stories about them: they clanged with authority above the dust-laden desert.

I gazed upward, neck craned back, feeling my mind and heart, loves and griefs sucked out into this circus of a sky. If I were not shivering already, I might have lain down on the sandy soil and surrendered to this wild ancient dance.

Taking a deep breath of cold night air, I turned to walk back to the women's dormitory, where I was ensconced in a tiny room like a nun's cell. And I took stock of my life. I was learning to be alone in the world, to take full responsibility for myself. I had moved again, into an apartment with a garden, where I felt I had entered a new life. At age sixty-three, I had a heightened sense of the shortness of the time ahead of me, and that unburdened me of much baggage from the past. There were some books I wanted to write, some places on the globe I wanted to visit. I hoped to stay as healthy as I was for many years to come. My heart was filled with gratitude for Ruth Denison and her teachings, for this place called Dhamma Dena, for the cancer that had taught me so much and for its absence now. And I remembered a moment the day before. During the holiday retreats, at the end of each morning session, Ruth plays a portion of a tape of Handel's *Messiah* sung in English. The day before, in this piece that commemorates the coming of the light in the darkness of winter, the soloist sang, "I know that my redeemer liveth," and tears began to stream down my face, for I understood the message for me, the knowledge of that luminous ground that underlies our lives and resides deep in each of us. My redeemer is that consciousness, that great ground of being into which we continually disappear and from which we are continually reborn.

Now in the black spangled desert night, at this place of effort and struggle, risk and safety, I realized that my life was finite, precious, and that if the cancer returned, I would try to meet it in the spirit of the Zen teacher Maurine Stuart, who said, "Whatever comes, don't make a move to avoid it."

And perhaps I'd come to the place in myself where I could wholeheartedly speak the words of Sono, ancient Shin Buddhist devotee: "Thanks for everything. I have no complaints whatsoever."

from

The Woman Within

ELLEN GLASGOW

In the past few years I have made a thrilling discovery, and in the past year I have had an even more thrilling adventure. My discovery was that until one is over sixty one can never really learn the secret of living. My adventure led me to the utmost border of death ("the ragged edge of eternity," my doctor called it) and kept me lingering, wholly conscious, without fear or reluctance or hesitation, in the kind of peace (or was it spiritual affirmation?) that passes both understanding and misunderstanding.

With the sardonic twist of circumstance, so prevalent in human affairs, I had no sooner learned how to live than the threat of death struck me. Only an Act of God, I used to boast, could ever kill me; but the one end I had not ever foreseen (for I had always said jestingly that my heart was too hard and cold to give way) was now approaching. Pain was barbed with surprise, because this particular pain was the last thing I had ever expected. "You have had no mercy on your heart," the specialist remarked solemnly, and I retorted, lightly, "My heart has never asked me for mercy."

It had taken me sixty years to discover that there was nothing to be done either about my own life or about the world in which I lived. All my fighting courage had brought to me was a badly damaged heart, yet a heart that was still undefeated. When the doctor told me this, I had a sudden uplifting sense of inward peace, of outward finality. I had done my best, and I could do nothing more. I had finished my course. I had kept the faith.

Youth is the season of tragedy and despair. Youth is the time when one's whole life is entangled in a web of identity, in a perpetual maze of seeking and of finding, of passion and of disillusion, of vague longings and of nameless griefs, of pity that is a blade in the heart, and of "all the little emptiness of love." Then the soul drifts on the shallow stream of personality, within narrow borders. Not until life has passed through that retarded channel out upon the wide open sea of impersonality, can one really begin to live, not simply with the intenser part of oneself, but with one's entire being. For sixty years, I was learning this elemental truth; and in the very moment of my discovery, I found also that the shadow I had imagined my own was the shadow of death.

Not that I greatly cared. Pain I had feared, but not death. The keenest pang was in the thought that I had fought all my life, and changed nothing. My old antagonist, inhumanity, was still victorious. All I had left behind me in life was a single endeavor. All the insurgent spirits that had so foolishly dreamed of destroying one evil or a multitude—what had they accomplished?

Two things had never failed me: my gift of friendship and my sense of laughter. In the tranquil years that followed, before the outbreak of a second World War, I filled my days with work, with friendship, with the familiar round of winters in Richmond and summers in Maine. It is true that I had never owned what I most wanted—a farm on which I could live through all seasons. I had never done what all my life I had wished to do—travel, alone, round the world.

But, if my traveling was over, I had seen, in the past, the world's lost age of beauty, before science, the soulless mother of invention, had devised the motor car, the tank, the diving bomb, the machine gun from the air, and all the barbarian mockery of a total civilized war. On some inward horizon, in immemorial loneliness, uninvaded by tourists, untroubled by motor horns, the Great Pyramids and the Sphinx stand forever against the blue noon, the flushed sunset, the silver night, and the paling sunrise over the desert. I had traveled for so many summers, in so many years. Everything I remembered was still my own. I had only to sink back into myself, to slip through some green door in the wall, and I could wander from Egypt to Greece, and over the Aegean Sea, in a cloudless dawn, to the glory of Smyrna.... I could ramble in the past for hours at a time. But I remind myself that, in autobiographies, I unfailingly skip all wandering parts.

I had nearly completed the first draft of my novel, which I had named *In This Our Life*, when the second World War broke. I cannot write of this war. I have tried, and I cannot.... The cruelty is too near. This cruelty is now in my mind. This agony is now in my nerves.

After both world wars are over, we shall still be fighting an eternal conflict between human beings and human nature. When this immediate evil power has been defeated, we shall not yet have won the long battle with the elemental barbarities. Another Hitler, it may be an invisible adversary, will attempt, again, and yet again, to destroy our frail civilization. Is it true, I wonder, that the only way to escape a war is to be in it? When one is a part of an actuality does the imagination find a release?

It is strange—or, perhaps, it is not strange—that war should reanimate the cruder, and more primitive, religious instincts. Someone, somewhere, is singing the hymn I hated and Father loved— poor Cowper's hymn—"There is a Fountain Filled with Blood." Over, and over, and over, until I shut out the sound by turning off my hearing device.... The blood symbolism in religion has always sickened me, in defiance of that stalwart breed, my Scottish forebears. I can feel this presence in the external atmosphere of a place, or, more vividly, through the air of my imagination. It is not alone the killing from which I recoil. I know that there are occasions when killing is necessary. But there is never a time when God or man, or the god invented by man, requires a libation of cruelty.

At the very beginning of the war in Europe, I did not feel the fullness of its impact all at once. Emotion, in common with all other mortal states or facts of nature, has an ultimate margin; it has an ebb and flow; it possesses the long finality of the dust. I had saturated my mind with the disturbed mental and emotional climate of my novel. I had completed, after my usual habit, the whole skeleton frame of *In This Our Life*. I had written this rapidly, passionately, straight from experience inflamed by imagination. Of all my later books I had written three drafts, the first for vitality and vividness of theme and of characterization, the second for arrangement and balance of scene and of structure, and the third for style and manner and the effort toward an unattainable perfection. By December, 1939, the first, and most difficult, writing was over, and of the second writing there remained only a short portion unfinished. After this would come a careful revision, and then the longest and final rewriting. Only a writer, it may be only a novelist, can understand how close this book, my last novel, had come to my heart. *In This Our Life* would bring the history in my long sequence of novels from 1850, the period in which *The Battle-Ground* opens, to the autumn of 1939. I was, moreover, approaching my subject, not from the single or even the dual point of view, but from the diffused mental and emotional outlook of a whole community. I felt that I was welding together, in this one symbolic expression, all the varied themes in my earlier and later interpretation of life.

I had reached this point when, in December, 1939, without

warning, my heart failed, and a mortal illness attacked me. I might, with care, I was told, live on for some years, or I might drop away in an hour, in a day, in a month, or in six months. Well, no matter. I might still have time to finish my novel. I might even finish my auto-biography. And so, as soon as the pain was over and I was able to sit up, I went back to my desk and my typewriter, and to four dozen new pencils with sharpened points. Though I had no fear of death, I did not like the thought of leaving a piece of good work, the topmost block in my building, unfinished.

For months I was able to work for only fifteen minutes, and a lit-tle later, half an hour every morning. Because this was not so much an act of creation as of rearrangement, enlargement, or elimination, the vitality of my novel would not, I felt, be impaired. By this time, the scene was permanently set; the living figures were all moving, and speaking in natural tones. This special effort, all the vital energy and motive power that a first writing exacts, would have been too much for me to demand from a failing heart. But I was dealing now not with dim outlines, but with well-rounded characters, as vigorous and alive as the human beings who went by in the street.

The winter passed, and I had completed my second writing, when I started for Castine, Maine, where I was spending my sum-mers. When I reached New York, the heart specialist there ordered me to a hospital.

I went reluctantly. "If I do not go, shall I have time to finish my book? I never like to leave work unfinished."

"How long will that take?"

"Until next winter. Maybe until November."

"You may and you may not. You may have six months. On the other hand you may have only three weeks. . . ." He had known me long enough to know that I wanted the truth.

So I left him to go to a gay and delightful luncheon in Emily

Balch's apartment on the East River. Later in the afternoon I went up to Doctors' Hospital, where I spent an endless month in all the intolerable sultry heat of New York. All through that July, I lay watching, from a high window, the slow boats and the misty green and the colored lights on the river.

For the first three weeks I was not allowed to see my friends; but they kept my room bright and fragrant with flowers, and for one week before I left, they came, in spite of the torrid weather, to spend hours by my bedside. "I may not like human nature," I would repeat, laughingly, to my delightful and devoted nurse, "but I like human beings."

At the end of the month I left for Castine. There I began to work again, and gradually to drive a little way, and then to walk, with Anne Virginia Bennett, for a quarter of a mile in the woods. But those heavenly rambles along the Indian trails were now over. In other years, after working from two to three hours every morning, I would start out and tramp in the woods until lunchtime. These walks had been my chief pleasure, and I began to hope that I might smell again the balsam over my head, and feel again the moss under my feet. But I had not been at Castine for more than three weeks when I came down with my worst heart attack, a coronary thrombosis. . . .

It is not possible to express, and especially to express in writing, the most profound experience that one has known—the recognition of death as another aspect of life. Millions of words have been written of dying; yet it is beyond the power of speech or of intelligence to describe the indescribable. Never again can I come so near the end of life without passing on into death. For nearly half an hour the Maine doctor watched, with his finger on my pulse and his stethoscope on my heart, and for every minute of that time I was completely conscious, but too weak to move my lips or flutter my eyelashes. I could see, fading slowly away, features of a kindly Roman senator bending over me. I could hear the voice of Anne Virginia calling to hold me back. I could see the face of my sister Rebe between the bed and the window. I could see the doctor's lips whispering, and though I could not hear his words, I knew that he said: "She is on the ragged edge. All we can do is to wait." Afterwards they told me he feared to give a second hypodermic, lest the shock of the needle might send me over that edge.... These things I remember or heard later; but these things are no more than the surface awareness, the thin shell of the moment. In my mind a single thought was repeated: If I cannot finish my book, I want to go quickly. After pain, there was no shadow of fear, of shrinking, or of reluctance. While an icy chill ran from my feet upward, it was, strangely enough, a chill that seemed the other side of a glow, of a warmth, as of an unutterable sense of fulfillment. I had never believed in a limited personal immortality, in a narrow margin of eternity or of the separate ego. The peace I felt was not the peace of possession. It was—the fleeting essence escapes whenever I try to confine it—a sense of infinite reunion with the Unknown Everything or with Nothing... or with God. But whether Everything or Nothing, it was surrender of identity.... By surrender, I do not mean extinction of identity. I mean, enlargement and complete illumination of being. In my death, as in my life, I was still seeking God, known or unknown....

Days afterward, I promised myself that I would never try to speak of what I could not put into words. All I knew was that I had looked at death, which is the other side of life, and that death was "lovely and soothing...." When I thought of dying, in those weary months of convalescence, it was not of dying as a cold negation, but as a warm and friendly welcome to the universe, to the Being beyond and above consciousness, or any vestige of self....

Yes, I have had my life. I have known ecstasy. I have known anguish. I have loved, and I have been loved. With one I loved, I have watched the light breaking over the Alps. If I have passed through "the dark night of the soul," I have had a far-off glimpse of the illumination beyond. For an infinitesimal point of time or eternity, I have caught a gleam, or imagined I caught a gleam, of the mystic vision. . . . It was enough, and it is now over. Not for everything that the world could give would I consent to live over my life unchanged, or to bring back, unchanged, my youth. . . .

Only on the surface of things have I ever trod the beaten path. So long as I could keep from hurting anyone else, I have lived, as completely as it was possible, the life of my choice. I have been free. Yet I have not ever stolen either the ponderable or the imponderable material of happiness. I have done the work I wished to do for the sake of that work alone. And I have come, at last, from the fleeting rebellion of youth into the steadfast—or is it merely the seasonable—accord without surrender of the unreconciled heart.

PART 2

Breaking Free

from

Aphrodite: A Memoir of the Senses

ISABEL ALLENDE

The fiftieth year of our life is like the last hour of dusk, when the sun has set and one turns naturally toward reflection.

In my case, however, dusk incites me to sin, and perhaps for that reason, in my fiftieth year I find myself reflecting on my relationship with food and eroticism; the weaknesses of the flesh that most tempt me are not, alas, those I have practiced most.

I repent of my diets, the delicious dishes rejected out of vanity, as much as I lament the opportunities for making love that I let go by because of pressing tasks or puritanical virtue. Walking through the gardens of memory, I discover that my recollections are associated with the senses.

My aunt Teresa, she who was slowly turning into an angel and died with buds of embryonic wings upon her shoulder blades, is linked forever with the scent of violet pastilles. When that enchanting lady came to visit, her gray dress discreetly highlighted by a lace collar and her snow-crowned head, we children would run to meet her and she, with ritual precision, would open a pocketbook worn slick with age—always the same one—and take out a small painted tin box from which she chose a mauve candy to hand to each of us. Ever since then, when the unmistakable scent of violets floats upon the air, the image of that sainted aunt, who stole flowers from others' gardens to take to dying inmates of the poorhouse, floods back into my heart, intact. Forty years later, I learned that the scent of violet was the cachet of Josephine Bonaparte, who trusted blindly in the aphrodisiac power of that evanescent aroma, a scent that suddenly assaults the senses with a nearly nauseating intensity only to disappear without a trace, then return with renewed ardor. Before their amorous encounters, the courtesans of ancient Greece used violet to perfume their breath and erogenous zones, because when blended with the natural odors of perspiration and feminine secretions, violet alleviates the melancholia of the eldest men and torments the young beyond endurance. In the Tantra, the mystical and spiritual philosophy that exalts the union of opposites at all levels, from the cosmic to the infinitesimal, and in which man and woman are mirrors of divine energies, violet is the color of female sexuality, which is why it has been adopted by some feminist movements.

For me, the penetrating odor of iodine stirs images not of wounds or surgeries, but of sea urchins, those strange creatures of the deep inevitably related to my initiation into the mystery of the senses. I was eight when the rough hand of a fisherman placed the tongue of a sea urchin in my mouth. When I visit Chile, I seek the opportunity to go to the coast and taste freshly caught sea urchins once more, and every time, I am flooded by the same mixture of terror and fascination I felt during that first intimate encounter with a man. Those ocean creatures are inseparable in my mind from that fisherman, with his dark sack of shellfish streaming seawater, and my awakening sensuality. That is how I remember all the men who have passed through my life—I don't want to boast, there aren't that many—some by the texture of their skin, others by the flavor of their kisses, the smell of their clothing, or the sound of their murmuring voice, and almost all of them are associated with some special food. The most intense carnal pleasure, enjoyed at leisure in a clandestine, rumpled bed, a perfect combination of caresses, laughter, and intellectual games, has the taste of a baguette, prosciutto, French cheese, and Rhine wine. With any of these treasures of cuisine, a particular man materializes before me, a long-ago lover who returns, persistent as a beloved ghost, to ignite a certain roguish fire in my mature years. That bread with ham and cheese brings back the essence of our embraces, and that German wine, the taste of his lips. I cannot separate eroticism from food and see no reason to do so. On the contrary, I want to go on enjoying both as long as strength and good humor last.

The road of gluttony leads straight to lust and, if traveled a little farther, to the loss of one's soul. This is why Lutherans, Calvinists, and other aspirants to Christian perfection eat so poorly. Catholics, on the other hand, who are born resigned to the concept of original sin and human frailty and who are purified by confession, free to go and sin again, are much more flexible in regard to the groaning board, so much so that the expression "a cardinal's tidbit" was coined to define something delicious. Lucky for me that I was brought up among the latter group and can devour as many treats as I wish with no thought of hell, only of my hips, although it has not been equally easy to shake off taboos relating to eroticism. I belong to the generation of women who married the first person with whom they "went all the way," because once their virginity was history, they were used goods on the matrimonial market, even though usually their partners were as inexperienced as they and seldom qualified to distinguish between virginity and prudery. If it weren't for the Pill, hippies, and women's lib, many of us would still be captives of obsessive monogamy.

In the Judeo-Christian culture, which divides the individual into body and soul, and love into profane and divine, anything having to do with sexuality, other than its reproductive function, is abominated. That demarcation was carried to the extreme when virtuous couples made love through an opening in the woman's nightgown embroidered in the form of a cross. Only the Vatican could imagine something that pornographic! In the rest of the world, sexuality is a component of good health; it inspires creation and is part of the pathway of the soul. It is not associated with guilt or secretiveness because sacred and profane love issue from the same source and it is supposed that the gods celebrate human pleasure. Unfortunately, it took me some thirty years to discover this. In Sanskrit the word that defines the joy of the creative principle is similar to the word for sensual bliss. In Tibet copulation is practiced as a spiritual exercise, and in Tantrism it is a form of meditation. The woman straddles the man, who is seated in the lotus position; they erase all thoughts from their mind, count their breaths, and lift their souls toward the divine, as their bodies join with tranquil elegance. Now, that makes you want to meditate.

Once an exquisite dinner has been prepared and served, once the secret warmth of the wine and tickle of the spices are coursing through the bloodstream and the anticipation of caresses turns the skin to a rosy glow, it is the moment to pause for a few minutes, postponing the encounter so that the lovers may regale each other with a story or a poem, as in the most refined traditions of the East. A story may also reawaken passion after the first enfolding, when lucidity and breath return and the couple is resting, well satisfied. Storytelling is a good way to keep the man awake, who tends to drop as if anesthetized, and to divert the woman when she begins to feel bored. That story or those verses are unique and precious: no one has told them or will ever tell them in that tone, at that rhythm, with that particular voice or precise intent. It isn't at all the same as a video, please, I beg you. If both lack a natural talent for making up stories, they can call upon the enormous, titillating repertoire of world literature, from the most exquisite erotic books to the most vulgar pornography—as long as it's kept to a minimum. The skill lies in prolonging pleasure by reading an exciting but brief excerpt; the amorous impetus won with the meal should not be misspent in literary excess. We are talking about how something as trivial as sex can be turned into an unforgettable occasion.

In my book *The Stories of Eva Luna,* there is a prologue that evokes the power of storytelling, something I couldn't have written had I not lived it. Forgive the arrogance of quoting myself, but I believe it illustrates my point. The lovers, Eva Luna and Rolf Carlé, are resting after impassioned lovemaking. In Rolf's photographic memory, the scene resembles an ancient painting in which a man's lover is lying beside him, her legs drawn up, a silk shawl over one shoulder, her skin still moist from love. Rolf describes the painting this way:

> *The man's eyes are closed; one hand is on his chest and the other on her thigh, in intimate complicity. That vision is recurrent and immutable; nothing changes: always the same peaceful smile on the man's face, always the woman's languor, the same folds in the sheets, the same dark corners of the room, always the lamplight strikes her breasts and cheekbones at the same angle, and always the silk shawl and the dark hair fall with the same delicacy.*
>
> *Every time I think of you, that is how I see you, how I see us, frozen for all time on that canvas, immune to the fading of memory. I spend immeasurable moments imagining myself in that scene, until I feel I am en-*

tering the space of the photograph and am no longer the man who observes but the man lying beside the woman. Then the quiet symmetry of the picture is broken and I hear voices very close to my ear.

"Tell me a story," I say to you.

"What about?"

"Tell me a story you have never told anyone before. Make it up for me."

A Song to Sensuality

MAYA ANGELOU

There is a cruel and stupid intolerance among the young. I know that is so because at the tender age of thirty I was given to declaim in injured tones: "Old women of fifty look awful in ropes of colored beads, thong sandals and fresh flowers in their hair" and "I've had it with old men [of fifty also] whose skin has gone to leather yet still wear open-neck shirts and heavy gold chains down to their crotches." I was not always careful whether or not the object of my derision could overhear me because I thought that if I spoke loudly maybe the old person would be lucky enough to learn something about proper dressing. Ah hah.

Ah hah, indeed. Now that I am firmly settled into my fifth decade, and pressing resolutely toward my sixth, I find nothing pleases me so much as gaudy outsized earrings, off-the-shoulder blouses and red hibiscus blooms pinned in my hair.

Do I look awful? Possibly to the young. Do I feel awful? Decidedly not. I have reached the lovely age where I can admit that sensuality satisfies me as much as sexuality and sometimes more so. I do not mean to suggest that standing on a hill in San Francisco, being buffeted by a fresh wind as I view the western sun setting into the bay will give me the same enjoyment as a night of lovemaking with the man of my fantasy. On the other hand, while the quantity of pleasure may weigh more heavily on the side of lovemaking, the quality between the two events is equal.

Leers and lascivious smirks to the contrary, sensuality does not necessarily lead to sex, nor is it meant to be a substitute for sex. Sensuality is its own reward.

There are some who are so frightened by the idea of sensual entertainment that they make even their dwelling places bleak and joyless. And what is horrible is that they would have others share that lonely landscape. Personally, I'll have no part of it. I want all my senses engaged.

I would have my ears filled with the world's music, the grunts of hewers of wood, the cackle of old folks sitting in the last sunlight and the whir of busy bees in the early morning. I want to hear the sharp sound of tap dancing and the mournful murmur of a spiritual half remembered and then half sung. I want the clashing cymbals of a marching band and the whisper of a lover entreating a beloved. Let me hear anxious parents warning their obstreperous offspring and a pedantic pedagogue teaching a bored class the mysteries of thermodynamics. All sounds of life and living, death and dying are welcome to my ears.

My eyes will gladly receive colors; the burnt-orange skin of old black women who ride on buses and the cool lavender of certain people's eyes. I like the tomato-red dresses of summer and the sienna of a highly waxed mahogany table. I love the dark green of rain forests and the sunshine yellow of a bowl of lemons. Let my eager sight rest on the thick black of a starless night and the crisp white of fresh linen. And I will have blue. The very pale blue of some complexions and the bold blue of flags. The iridescent blue of hummingbird wings and the dusty blue of twilight in North Carolina. I am not daunted by the blood-red of birth and the red blood of death. My eyes absorb the world's variety and uniqueness.

Taste and smell are firmly joined in wedded bliss. About the bliss I cannot speak, but I can say much about that marriage. I like it that the fleeting scent of fresh-cut citrus and the flowery aroma of strawberries will make my salivary glands pour into my mouth a warm and pure liquid. I accept the salt of tears evoked by sweet onions and betrayed love. Give me the smell of the sea and the wild scent of mountain pines. I do not spurn the suffocating smell of burned rubber of city streets nor the scent of fresh sweat because their pungency reminds me of the bitterness of chocolate and the sting of vinegar. Some of life's greatest pleasures are conveyed by the dual senses of taste and smell.

In this tribute to sensuality I have saved the sense of touch as the last pleasure to be extolled. I wish for the slick feel of silk underclothes and the pinch of sand in my beach shoes. I welcome the sun strong on my back and the tender pelting of snow on my face. Good clothes that fit snugly without squeezing and strong fearless hands that caress without pain. I want the crunch of hazelnuts between my teeth and ice cream melting on my tongue.

I will have that night of sexuality with the man who inhabits my fantasy. I'll take the sensuality and the sexuality. Who made the rule that one must choose either or?

from

Revolution from Within

GLORIA STEINEM

๖๑

*We grow neither better nor worse as
we get old, but more like ourselves.*

MARY LAMBERTON BECKER

Dorothy Dinnerstein, the sociologist and author of *The Mermaid and the Minotaur,* once said that growing up in a family teaches us two crucial things: how to get along with and love people who don't share our interests, and what to expect from the various stages of life.

I was struck by the wisdom of the first part of her remark and bored by the second. Didn't everyone know about "the stages of life"?

Well, everything sounds trite before we're ready for it. Almost two decades later, I realized I didn't understand the process of aging at all. Thanks to my very small family, the patterns of my parents' lives, and the fact that I've worked mostly in movements where age differences melt in a furnace of shared interests, I had never thought about or lived with the surprising, upsetting, implacable, and irrevocable mystery of aging. Instead, I had been behaving as if the long plateau of an activist middle of life went on forever.

Though my circumstances set me apart from many of my friends

—for instance, I hadn't chosen to have children and so didn't have their growth as a measure of time—I discovered that few people I knew had a vision of anything but a cliff at the end of this plateau. The rarity of extended families, the lack of multigenerational communities, and too few media images that extend beyond forty or fifty—all these things had stopped our imaginations. Meanwhile, my apparent belief that I was immortal, with all the time in the world, was causing me to plan poorly—to put it mildly.

Fortunately, our bodies are great teachers: even their smallest intimations of mortality are shocks we never forget. I remember having my hair washed at a shop in another city, apologizing as usual for having long hair that is time-consuming to dry, and being told cheerfully, "That's okay—it's rather thin." Then there was the moment when I realized I could only count on going sleepless for one night—not two—when I needed to meet a deadline. And my always nearsighted eyes began to get farsighted at the same time. "I always thought my patients were exaggerating," the optician said when I asked him if I was going blind or just aging, "until I passed forty—now I know exactly what you mean."

These bodily signals sent me into the first stage of dealing with aging: denial. I was going to continue living *exactly as I always had*—and make a virtue of it. If age were ever to interrupt sexual life, for instance, I would just continue it in a different way. After all, the world could use a pioneer dirty old lady. Dorothy Pitman Hughes and I began fantasizing a future as bawdy old women sitting on bar stools in skirts that were too tight, sending out for an occasional young sailor. (Of course, neither one of us drank, or felt attracted to members of the opposite sex who hadn't lived through at least some of the same history—but the fact that dirty old men were almost our only role models was a measure of how finite we felt our options to be.) If I ever grew too infirm to work and my delusions of perpetual youth had still prevented me from saving any money, then I would just become a bag lady. It was a life like any other, and I could always help organize the other bag ladies.

Gradually, this first stage of denial blended into a second, more energized one: defiance. Two of my role models for this future were George Burns, who had just signed a contract to play the Palladium in London on his hundredth birthday (he was well into his eighties at the time, a bravado which made me overlook his not-so-great sex jokes about young women), and Ruth Gordon, who wore miniskirts in her eighties, had a younger husband (playwright Garson Kanin), and acted up a storm in movies (remember *Harold and Maude*?). She also said satisfying things like "I think there is one smashing rule: Never face the facts."

In this spirit, I celebrated my fiftieth birthday in a very public way by turning it into a feminist benefit (which I hope my funeral will also be), and tried to offer some encouragement to other women facing the double standard of aging by getting as far out of the age closet as possible. Of course, I continued to hear "fifty" as old when applied to other people and had consciously and constantly to revise my own assumptions. Though I began making an effort to use time better and to understand that my life wasn't going to go on forever— that is, to use turning fifty to good purposes—my heart wasn't in it. In fact, I didn't revise one single thing about my living habits: no exercise except running through airports; no change in my sugar-addicted eating habits; no admission that this long plateau in the middle of my life might be leading into new terrain. In a way, I felt I *couldn't* acknowledge limitations or any of the weaknesses to which the flesh is heir; the everyday emergencies of a magazine and a movement were all-consuming, and I didn't think I could stop swimming in midstream. But to a larger degree, I just didn't know how. I didn't have a model of how to get from here to there; from where I was to seventy, eighty, and hopefully beyond. I needed a model not of *being old*, but of *aging*.

Thanks to good genes, I got away with all this defiance for quite a while—which may be exactly why I needed the word *cancer* to come into my life. Nothing less than such a bodily warning would have made me think about the way I was living. Sleeplessness and endless stress, a quart of ice cream at a time, and my lifetime rule of no exercise: I was so unaccustomed to listening to any kind of messages from within that I'd ceased to be able to hear even a whisper from that internal voice that must ultimately be our guide. In fact, I had no patience at all with anyone who suggested it was there to be listened to.

Cancer changed that. It gave me a much-needed warning, and it taught me something else: it was not death I had been defying. On the contrary, when I got this totally unexpected diagnosis, my first thought was a bemused, "So this is how it's all going to end." My second was, "I've had a wonderful life." Such acceptance may sound odd, but I felt those words in every last cell of my being. It was a moment I won't forget.

Eventually, that diagnosis and my reaction to it made me realize that I'd been worrying about aging; that my denial and defiance were related to giving up a way of being, not ceasing to be. Though I would have decried all the actresses, athletes, and other worshipers of youth who were unable to imagine a changed future—a few of whom have even chosen death *over* aging—I had been falling into the same trap.

For this health warning—plus the dawning of an understanding that to fear aging is really to fear a new stage of life—I was fortunate to pay only a small price. Thanks to the impact of the women's health movement on at least some of the health-care system, my treatment consisted of a Novocain shot and a biopsy at a women's clinic, while I watched an infinitesimal lump being removed in what turned out to be its entirety—rather like taking out an oddly placed splinter. Since the mammogram had shown nothing—15 percent show false negatives, which is another reason for self-examination—the diagnosis of malignancy was a shock. But what came after was not nearly as difficult as what many women have faced. First, there was a lymph-node sampling that did require going into a hospital, but didn't interfere with going dancing the evening I got out. Since the sampling was negative, the rest of the treatment consisted of six weeks of lying like the Bride of Frankenstein on a metal slab each morning while I got radiation treatments. My self-treatment was much more drastic: doing away with all animal fat in my diet and getting less stress and more sleep. All this has helped me remain cancer free for the last five years.

Nonetheless, I was frightened enough by this timely warning to start doing what I needed to do, indeed what I should have been doing all along: listening to what my physical self had to say. Perhaps one of the rewards of aging is a less forgiving body that transmits its warnings faster—not as betrayal, but as wisdom. Cancer makes one listen more carefully, too. I began to seek out a healthier routine, a little introspection, and the time to do my own writing. . . .

For me thus far, the only disappointment with this new country called aging is that it hasn't liberated me from that epithet of "the pretty one"—though in the past, I sometimes pleasurably fantasized about getting old to get rid of it. If that sounds odd, think about working as hard as you can, and then discovering that whatever you accomplish is attributed to your looks. The upside has been a better understanding of women who really are great beauties—not just feminists who don't fit a media stereotype—and who are treated without reference to their inner reality, as well as denied sympathy. Perhaps a more personal upside is seeing age as freedom.

In my current stage of aging and listening, I've learned the importance of starting with the body and all its senses. Which is why I go to my body to ask what this new country of aging will be like.

I look at my hands, of which I am so proud, for instance, and seeing their backs sprinkled with small brown age spots is shocking at first. So I ask them what they have to say for themselves. "A banner held in liver-spotted hands," they reply. I get a title for a future article, plus my first inkling that liver spots have a sense of humor.

I notice that the hormonal changes of menopause seem to have freed a part of my brain once preoccupied with sex—thus bringing a more relaxed, I-enjoy-it-when-it-happens-but-don't-obsess-about-it attitude—so I ask these brain cells what they're planning to do with the extra time. "Celebrate not being stuck with bars and sailors," they say. Suddenly, I feel liberated.

I wonder if I should let the bleached streaks in my hair grow out after all these years. I don't want to put "a ceiling on my brain," as Alice Walker would say. Then the phrase "punk-rock purple" comes out of nowhere. Maybe even aging hair doesn't have to be serious.

Looking in the mirror, I see the lines between nose and mouth that now remain, even without a smile, and I am reminded of a chipmunk storing nuts for the winter. This is the updated version of my plump-faced child. When I ask what they have to say for themselves, nothing comes back. They know I don't like them, so until I stop with the chipmunk imagery and learn to value them as the result of many smiles, they're not communicating. I'll have to work on this—and many other adjustments of aging still to come.

But I have a new role model for this adventurous new country I'm now entering. She is a very old, smiling, wrinkled, rosy, beautiful woman, standing in the morning light of a park in Beijing. Her snow-white hair is just visible under a jaunty lavender babushka. Jan Phillips, who took her photograph, says she was belting out a Chinese opera to the sky, stopped for a moment to smile at the camera, and then went on singing. Now, she smiles at me every morning from my mantel.

I love this woman. I like to think that, walking on the path ahead of me, she looks a lot like my future self.

from

The Change

GERMAINE GREER

When Karen Blixen was forty-six she came out of Africa back to Denmark. Her coffee plantation in Kenya had gone broke; though it was auctioned off to pay the accumulated debts, the stockholders lost more than £150,000. Her unfaithful husband, whom she had forgiven for giving her syphilis, had insisted on a divorce, which she had agreed to with reluctance. All her hopes of pregnancy had been dashed, and she had quarreled with her lover, who was killed in a plane crash days later. She had attempted suicide at least once during this turbulent tune. She was so thin and frail that her friends had suggested that she go to a clinic in Montreux; there she found out that her syphilis, which had been supposed cured, had become syphilis of the spine, *tabes dorsalis.* The course of the disease was well known; locomotor ataxia meant she would never again walk properly, anorexia meant that food would nauseate her, she would develop perforating stomach ulcers, and her face would soon take on a deadly pallor and be covered with a grid of tight wrinkles. Her greatest bereavement was the loss of Africa, which left her with a physical longing for the light, the sky and the bush that never faded. Crates of treasured possessions followed her to Denmark, but she did not open them for thirteen years.

Baroness Blixen's way of dealing with her intense physical and mental pain at this crisis time...was to be reborn as Isak Dinesen. Isaac was the postmenopausal child of Abraham and Sarah, who said when he was born, "God hath made me to laugh, so that all that hear will laugh with me." Dinesen was Blixen's maiden name. She herself called this time her fourth age, saying she began to write "in great uncertainty about the whole undertaking, but, nevertheless, in the hands of both a powerful and happy spirit."

Out of Africa is about the Africa she lost, and with it the love, hope, health and light that she would never know again; it is imbued with the elegiac feeling that is the reward for having been able to mourn and to let go. Hannah Arendt explains the importance of storytelling in Blixen's struggle to defy her dreadful illness:

> *Without repeating life in imagination you can never be fully alive, "lack of imagination" prevents people from "existing." "Be loyal to the story," as one of her storytellers admonishes the young...means no less than, Be loyal to life, don't create fiction but accept what life is giving you, show yourself worthy of whatever it may be by recollecting and pondering over it, thus repeating it in imagination; this is the way to remain alive. And to live in the sense of being fully alive had early been and remained to the end her only aim and desire. "My life, I will not let you go except you bless me, but then I will let you go." The reward of storytelling is to be able to let go: "When the storyteller is loyal...to the story, there, in the end, silence will speak."*

Karen Blixen exerted her old woman's power many times, enchanting several younger and stronger men into acting out her fantasies for years at a time. In these relationships, although she did not permit herself physical intimacy, she was as exacting as any lover. Using her emaciated appearance and her stark-white, fantastically wrinkled pixie face, with its huge, glittering, kohl-encircled eyes, she fascinated her prey and kept them subject to her whims by binding them fast with the yarns she spun. Racked by her cruel disease, Karen Blixen remains a virtuosa of the art of aging.

———

Karen Blixen used to say, "One must in this lower world love many things to know finally what one loves the best...." It is simply not true that the aging heart forgets how to love or becomes incapable of love; indeed, it seems as if, at least in the case of...women of great psychic energy, only after they had ceased to be beset by the egotisms and hostilities of sexual passion did they discover of what bottomless and tireless love their hearts were capable.

———

The woman ejected from feminine subjection by the consequences of her own aging can no longer live through others, or justify her life by the sexual and domestic services that she renders. She must, being in free fall, take a long look at the whole landscape that surrounds her and decide how she is going to manage to live in it, no matter how chill the wind that buffets her ill-equipped person. At first she may cling to her old life, trying to claw back something of what she poured into it so unstintingly, but eventually, her grieving done, her outrage stilled, she must let go. Only if she lets go can she recover her lost potency. The younger woman needs her love objects too desperately to love them without hostility in an undestructive way. When the older woman releases or is forced to release her desperate stranglehold and feels herself dropping away, real love will bear her up.

———

Once we lose our sense of grievance everything, including physical pain, becomes easier to bear. As the inflammatory response in the body slows down, so does the inflammation of the mind. As we hoist in the fact that happiness is not something we are entitled to, or even something we are programmed for, we begin to understand that there is no virtue in being miserable. We can then begin to strive for the heroism of real joy.

—

The lifting up of the heart is a strenuous business and we must work our way into it gradually. This is not a joy that comes from lack of awareness or refusal to contemplate the pain of the world. It comes from the recognition of the bitterness of the struggle, not just for ourselves, but for everyone, and the importance of survival. When silly death wishes and juvenile self-destructiveness are at length driven out, the spiritual athlete can pile on the weights and smile genuinely in her own triumph over a nobler kind of pain than the pangs of self-pity that once beset her.

—

The discontent of youth passes when you realize that the music you are hearing is not about you, but about itself. The important thing is not you listening to the music, but the self-realizing form of the music itself. Then you can begin to understand that beauty is not to be found in objects of desire but in those things that exist beyond desire, that cannot be subordinated to any use that human beings can make of them.

—

Only when a woman ceases the fretful struggle to *be* beautiful can she turn her gaze outward, find the beautiful and feed upon it. She can at last transcend the body that was what other people principally valued her for, and be set free both from their expectations and her own capitulation to them. It is quite impossible to explain to younger women that this new invisibility, like calm and indifference, is a desirable condition. At first even the changing woman herself protests against it; she may even take steps to reverse it, by wearing more revealing or garish clothes, but sooner or later she will be forced to accept it. Some of the evidence seems to show that women who have been shortchanged by our education system, so that their minds are undeveloped and their imaginations unstimulated, never manage this transition but remain blind and embittered. When they are at the mercy of a mass culture that celebrates older women who "still remain youthful" and spend enormous sums of money in the attempt to fashion themselves into ghastly simulacra of youthful bodies, they have less chance than ever of surmounting the shock of invisibility.

Religion is one of the easier ways that the aging woman can unlock the door to her interior life. If she has been an unreflective Christian or Hindu or Muslim or Jew or Buddhist she may find it easiest to find her interior life by entering more deeply into the implications of her religion. Examples of the piety of older women are to be seen on all sides; what is not so easy to discern is the joy that entering into the intellectual edifices of the great religions can give, to those who have faith. Women who do not adhere to a particular creed will nevertheless find that in the last third of their lives they come to partake of the "oceanic experience" as the grandeur and the pity of human life begin to become apparent to them. As one by one the Lilliputian strings that tie the soul down to self-interest and the short view begin to snap the soul rises higher and higher, until the last one snaps, and it floats free at last. That last string is probably the string of life itself, but you must not ask me to be more precise. My own gyves have only just begun to fall away—I cannot see so far.

Let younger people anxiously inquire, let researchers tie themselves in knots with definitions that refuse to stick, the middle-aged woman is about her own business, which is none of theirs. Let the Masters in Menopause congregate in luxury hotels all over the world to deliver and to hearken to papers on the latest astonishing discoveries about the decline of grip strength in menopause or the number of stromal cells in the fifty-year-old ovary, the woman herself is too busy to listen. She is climbing her own mountain, in search of her own horizon, after years of being absorbed in the struggles of others. The way is hard, and she stumbles many times, but for once no one is scrambling after her, begging her to turn back. The air grows thin, and she may often feel dizzy. Sometimes the weariness spreads from her aching bones to her heart and brain, but she knows that, when she has scrambled up this last sheer obstacle, she will see how to handle the rest of her long life.

On Being a Rebellious Old Woman

BABA COOPER

I live in Vacation Land. Come summer, Main Street is bumper to bumper with RVs filled with aging tourists. True, the lines of foam breaking the indigo of the sea against the pine tufted cliffs attract all ages of city folk, searching for places where Nature is still winning over tourism. But a lot of the people here aren't vacationers; they are retirees, old people like me, come to live full-time in their vacation homes. Lots of old men, with their middle-aged wives in tow. Sport fishermen, pulling boats behind their Winnebagos, burdened with all their equipment. The local Safeway has lots of wide spaces in the parking lot marked "RV ONLY." I go to Safeway more to study my contemporaries than to benefit from the dubious specials. In the long lines of the computer-equipped checkout stands, I can stare with impunity at the living norms of my generation—norms untouched by poverty or racial differences—Americans who have made it into the golden years.

Why am I so curious about a group I should know as well as anyone, being one of them? I am not poor; I live in a lovely little house near the sea, crafted by me to fit exactly the needs of my later years. I am white and able-bodied. But I don't fit the norm. Months, sometimes even years, go by without my seeing a woman I can identify with—one who signals resistance to the role fulfillment expected of my age/sex bracket. Nor do I find them in TV or advertisements or the movies. Even more disturbing is the absence of my image in books. Until the strong, honest face of Barbara Macdonald accosted me from the cover of *Look Me in the Eye*,[1] and I found words inside that book that matched some of my experience, it was possible to view myself as one of a kind, unique.

What is so strange about me? I am a woman like hundreds of others I know who is trying to tinker with my life choices—to fit them as best I can to what I have learned from feminist analysis. I am simply a woman saying *no* to some patriarchal expectations and conditioning. I say *no* to the extent that I am able to refuse without threatening my basic survival. Unfortunately, other women like me are young, whereas I am old. The rebellious young share signals of their mutiny with other women of their own age. They have not thought about the possibility of a rebellious old woman. In fact, to the extent that older women are part of their support system, their stability, the base they can exploit as they wrestle their due from the Fathers, they are not really ready for me. I become an exception.

If there is any position I fear, it is that of the exceptional woman. In my preliberation days, I hid a lot from myself by believing that I was an exception—exceptionally gifted and exceptionally difficult. I was flattered when someone told me I thought like a man. Now I would be insulted. But again, as I have grown older and more radical, it becomes convenient to slip into personalizing the politics of my situation.

For instance, I am a grandmother. My struggles to make my married daughters understand that I must relate to this role differently—or not at all—have failed miserably. No one is interested in my need for negotiation.

How do we change? Am I alone in questioning the assumptions about my time, my affections, my willingness to buy or bribe allegiance, the availability of my services and space? I have raised four children; my mothering instincts are worn exceedingly thin. Why is it up to me to bear the brunt of refusal, withdrawal? With so many grandmothers in the world, am I the only one who wants things to be different?

Recently I read about the revolutionary heroine of Nicaragua's Foreign Ministry, a lawyer and single mother of five. In the view of the writer as well as the revolutionary herself, she is a feminist. Since a busy career leaves her little time for her children, "her widowed mother takes care of them." It is much the same in the Soviet Union and China, where revolution has opened up opportunities for younger women, taking them out of the home while grandmothers are expected to pick up the slack. In China the grandmothers now will have only one grandchild to raise because of the decrees of the Fathers, while in Nicaragua and the Soviet Union, the state controls female reproduction in the other direction, by withholding abortion and contraceptive information. This is socialist feminist progress?

First the men unload responsibility for their children upon women, then women become liberated and unload their children on their old mothers. It is quite irrelevant that there are ethnic, religious, and class taboos against anything but joyful acceptance of these expectations in the old women themselves. Liberation for women means old women too. I know that these grandmothers are often the ones who insist that they want to do what they are doing, who resist the attempts of governments to limit births, who insist that grandchildren give them a reason for living. I also recognize that the old women in the United States often unwillingly live far away from their grandchildren. None of this legitimizes exploiting old women in unpaid jobs that repeat the stresses of their child-rearing years. Service is not necessarily the *function* of age in women.

When I came out at fifty-one, it was my hope to escape from the pernicious roles and expectations of heterosexuality into a world where my goal would be personal growth. I wanted my personal choices to be politicized by the question "Who profits and who loses from this?" I wanted to fashion my relationships so that neither I nor another would be used—that elusive utopia of equality within intimacy. Although I am not adverse to nurturing others, I want my last years to reflect personal potentials that were suppressed in me as a young and midlife woman. It is important to me that I do not submerge my identity in any female service role, least of all with my grandchildren.

1. Barbara Macdonald and Cynthia Rich, *Look Me in the Eye: Old Women, Aging, and Ageism* (San Francisco: Spinsters, Ink, 1983).

Upstaging Time

GRACE PALEY

I must tell you that at the first upsurge of a contentious or merely complicated concern, I'm likely to slip into a fictional mode. This is a way of thinking, a habit of thought.

For example: A couple of years ago a small boy yelled out as he threw a ball to a smaller boy standing near me, "Hey, dummy, tell that old lady to watch out."

What? What lady? Old? I'm not vain or unrealistic. For the last twenty years my mirror seems to have reflected—correctly —a woman getting older, not a woman old. Therefore, I took a couple of the hops, skips, and jumps my head is accustomed to making and began to write what would probably become a story. The first sentence is: "That year all the boys on my block were sixty-seven."

Then I was busy and my disposition, which tends to crude optimism anyway, changed the subject. Also, my sister would call, and from time to time she'd say, "Can you believe it? I'm almost seventy-eight. And Vic is going on eighty. Can you believe it?" No, I couldn't believe it, and neither could anyone who talked to them or saw them. They've always been about fifteen years older than I, and still were. With such a sister and brother preceding me, it would seem bad manners to become old. My aging (the aging of the youngest) must seem awfully pushy to them.

Actually, they're both so deep into music, archaeology, Russian conversation lessons, botany, tutoring high school students, writing, and remembering for grandchildren and great-nephews and -nieces the story of their Russian-language childhood on Chrystie Street and later in Harlem that they may not notice me trailing them at all.

By the time I returned to that first sentence, the boys had become sixty-nine. Most of them were in decent shape, nice-looking older men—those boys whose war was World War II. (There is a war for every boy—usually given by his father's generation.)

But two of them were no longer present, having leapt out of the air of the world into the actuarial statistics that insurance companies keep, where men, in death as in life, have a sad edge over women, often leaving them years of widowhood. (This is pointed out to us in a kind of accusatory way, as though this new longevity is due to a particular selfishness on our part—female life-greed.) The fact is that women may well be owed a couple of years of extra time, historically speaking, since our deaths as young women in various ritual torments and in childbirth are well known. The great men of history, it is recorded, have often been forced to use more than one wife —serially speaking—in order to properly and sufficiently reproduce themselves. This was sometimes unpleasant for them, too, though not always.

In spite of this parenthetical interruption I returned to my work and was able to write the next sentence of what may still become a story: "Two years later, two of the boys had died and my husband said, 'Well, I'd better take this old-age business a little more seriously.'" So we did.

[Poem to Prove Seriousness]

Questions

Do you think old people should be put away?
the one red rheumy eye the pupil goes back
and back
the hands are scaly
do you think all that should be hidden

do you think young people should be seen
so much on Saturday night
hunting and singing in packs the way they do
standing on street corners looking this way
and that

or the small children who are visible all the time
everywhere
and have nothing to do but be smart
but be athletes
but jump
but climb high fences
do you think hearts should sink
do you think the arteries ought to crumble
when they could do good
because the heart was made to endure
why does it not endure?
do you think this is the way it should be?

DIALOGUE
Don't you think that poem was kind of gloomy?
But don't you have to be truthful?

There's more to getting older than that. What about friendship? All that special energy—you've written about it yourself. What about experience and wisdom?
But did you really want me to say it was all okay and zippy? Still, you may be right, a little bit. Because for me, I'm well, my children are well, my stepchildren are well. And as I pointed out, even my oldest siblings, with terrifying surgical memories and arteries sticky with the bakeries of the Upper West Side, offer high examples of liveliness, interest in the world, and hope for tomorrow. This is proven by purchases of long season subscriptions to concerts and ballets and the determination to proceed to those events with whatever spiritual and physical equipment is working. So you are right. Several years ago my sister bought me, for my fifty-fifth birthday, ten Arthur Murray ballroom dancing lessons with her favorite partner.

Okay, so now you agree that poem was gloomy.
You're right, and you're wrong, and anyway, that's not the point. The point is that if you insist on saying that old age is only a slightly different marketplace of good looks, energy, and love, you insult lots of others. For instance, I'm not poor. I'm a white woman in a middle-class life, and even there some luck usually has to apply. Also, when I need to knock wood I can just run out my door to a little forest of maple and hemlock to knock on the best living wood for my luck. Also, I'm not alone in this world, I'm not without decent shelter.

All right, I see what you're saying. But people do need to be encouraged. Why won't you admit it? We only want you to be a little upbeat. It's not against your nature.
Okay. I'll try from now on. But I might, just once, slip.

THE RELATIVITY OF AGE

About sixteen years ago at the beginning of the energetic prime of my fifties, in Chile, in the town of Quillota, a few months before the Pinochet coup, the death of Allende, we met a man with an attaché case full of American bills. He was a trucker with a small pickup. "Come to my house," he said, loving Americans. "Here's a picture of my children. I had fourteen. Twelve live."

We came to his dusty courtyard, on which the American cash had not yet gone to work. "This is my beautiful daughter," he said, introducing us. "She's eighteen. That's my wife." He pointed to an old woman leaning on the outdoor washbasin. She turned away. "Sick," he said. She was thirty-five years old.

In an honest effort to cheer up I asked one of my students to interview any older woman who happened to be passing the stoop where she and I were sitting talking about the apartment situation in New York. She was the kind of kid who's loaded with initiative. She began at once:

Student Interviewer: Excuse me, ma'am. How do you keep busy?

Older Woman: What do you mean by that? I work. I have to keep my place decent. I take care of my aunt. Her kids moved to California. By the way, you don't seem to be doing too much yourself except interfering with us promenaders.

S.I.: Do you *feel* old?

O.W.: Well, middle age in this country comes so late, if it wasn't for the half fares, I'd never give it up.

S.I.: Do you have many friends?

O.W.: Well, I guess I do. We've been meaning to get together and have this group—this women's group on getting older. You know, everything that happens—some things are interesting and some things are not so hot. But the truth is, we're too busy. Every time we say we're going to get it together, two people have a long job to finish. It's a good idea, though.

S.I.: Do you live with your family?

O.W.: My family doesn't live with *me*. They already have lived with me a number of years.

S.I.: Who do you live with?

O.W.: My lover.

S.I.: Oh. So you're still interested in sex, that means.

O.W.: Yes, I am.

S.I. *(shyly)*: Would you elaborate?

O.W.: Not to you.

WHAT IT'S LIKE

You may begin to notice that you're invisible. Especially if you're short and gray-haired. But I say to whom? And so what? All the best minorities have suffered that and are rising nowadays in the joy of righteous wrath.

Some young people will grab your elbow annoyingly to help you off and on the curb at least fifteen years before you'd want them to.

Just tell them, "Hands off, kiddy." Some others with experience in factional political disputes fear the accusation of ageism and, depending on their character, either defer to you with a kind look or treat you cruelly as an equal. On the other hand, people do expect wise and useful remarks—so, naturally, you offer them. This is called the wisdom of the old. It uses clichés the way they ought to be used, as the absolute truth that time and continuous employment have conferred on them.

You are expected to be forgetful. You are. At least as forgetful as you have always been. For instance, you lose your eyeglasses. You have lost your eyeglasses all your life. You have lost your keys, as well as other people's, frequently. It was once considered a charming if expensive eccentricity, proving that your head was in the literary clouds it was supposed to be in. Your family is not too rude, but you don't like the way they look at each other. Pretty soon you stop mislaying your keys—not altogether, but enough to prove you could have always done so.

You are expected to forget words or names, and you do. You may look up at the ceiling. People don't like this. They may say, "Oh come on, you're not listening." You're actually trying to remember their names.

While he could still make explanations, my father explained to me that the little brain twigs, along with other damp parts of the body, dry up, but that there is still an infinity of synaptic opportunities in the brain. If you forget the word for peach ("A wonderful fruit," he said), you can make other pathways for the peach picture. You can attach it to another word or context, which will then return you to the word "peach," such as "What a peachy *friend*," or springtime and peach *blossoms*. This is valuable advice, by the way. It works. Even if you're only thirty, write it down for later.

My father wanted—in general—to tell me how to grow old. I

thought that the restoration of those lost words was almost enough, but he had also taken a stand against wrinkles. He applied creams assiduously to the corners of his mouth and his heels. I did not, when I could, pay enough attention, and now I'm sorry, though it's probably a scientific fact that your genes have got you by the shortening muscles of your throat as well as the number of hairs time leaves on your head.

Soon it was too late to ask him important questions and our conversations happened in the world where people say, "Is that a story or a fact?"

A STORY OR A FACT

He had fallen, hurt his head, where time is stored. When he spoke, he made the most direct connections. If I listened, I heard his mind taking the simplest synaptic opportunity and making a kind of poem in that necessity. Follow him for a moment, please.

"Come into the room," my father called to me, "come into the room. I have located your second husband," he said. "I have just located him. Not only his body, but his mind. We talked over there on the couch. Does he want my money? Why does he think he can wear old clothes? I have an extra suit. Give it to him. Well, this is the way we are made—getting old—the problem of old men. The problem of old women—we can talk about that later; I'm not interested.

"Do you know these women? The ones I live with in this house. The one who makes my supper, the one that lives in someone's room—the person that's missing. (I told you someone very important was missing. Who? Mama?) Last night they made a party. Very wild music. Not unpleasant, but not usual. Some others came. Men who talked nicely. The women invited me to their party and they said why not dance; they offered me a chance to—well, you know what. I said to them, 'Can't you see how old I am.' Look, I told them they were very handsome women, not to be insulted. But I'm old. I had to explain to them. Feelings can be hurt." Old, he said. Without sadness, but apologetically, as though it were an offense, not the sorrow of human life.

Interviewer: Why did you tell me this story?

Grace: Because I saw you bought a stunning new winter coat and were about to become too sentimental.

Interviewer: Why are you so hard?

Grace: Well, am I? You do have to come out of late middle age into this older time with your muscles of imagination in good shape, and your muscles of swimming against the tides of misinformation pretty strong—as well as the usual back and abdominal muscles, which are kind of easy to exercise in the morning.

Interviewer: You're not so easy to deal with.

Grace: Why should I be? Like most people my age, I've accumulated enough experience to be easy or difficult, whatever the provocation exacts. Your trouble is you don't have a gift, or the character, for normal tragedy.

Interviewer: That's not really fair. I suppose I have to let it go at that, but I do have a few fairly simple questions I'd like to ask you. What have you liked about your life?

Grace: I've liked being Jewish. I've liked being a woman. When I was a little girl, I liked thinking I was a boy. I loved growing up in

New York City, the Bronx, my street—and I've tried to give those advantages to my children.

Interviewer: What do you miss?

Grace: My mother, who died before we had all the good talks that are now in books, thanks to the women's movement. I miss my children's childhood. Now that I live in the country, which I love, I miss my political, grass-roots life in the New York streets. Vigiling in a shopping center in New Hampshire is not quite the same.

Interviewer: Do you mind having to get older?

Grace *(somewhat annoyed, but luckily slips into another story)*: When I was twelve and a half, I was walking along Southern Boulevard in the Bronx on the way to the Elsemere movie house with a boy named David, with whom I was in love. He was fourteen and very sophisticated. "What do you think is the greatest age for a woman?" he asked. I pretended to think, though I already knew. "Eighteen," I said. "Oh no," he sighed, "twenty-six, twenty-six—that's the age a woman should be." "That old?" I asked. "That's awful. It's disgusting." David looked at me as though he had never noticed how young I was. He dropped my hand.

By the way, my answer to your question is, I feel great. I like my life a lot. It's interesting every day. But it so happens I *do* mind.

Nana I Ke Ku …
Looking to the Source

YVONNE MOKIHANA CALIZAR

I don't say we're old, but some say it. "We're at that age," they say. What age is that, anyway? Middle age, half-moon age. When old friends gather and widen the circle of stones to include their daughters, the question of age becomes a fuller story. The wisdom of having lived stretches the limits of younger expectations. Things from the "sometime in my life I'm gonna" list becomes "what's happening now."

I laugh as Michele and I drive off in her rental Mustang, waving to Nola's only child. She peeks out through the opened louvers of her tiny cottage and giggles at us. "That looks so cool." It's not as though one ride in a red Mustang convertible turns this pair of *Pake*-Hawaiian *wahine* into candidates for the Thelma and Louise gallery. But it does give us both memories of another great time together, doing stuff that we could not create separately.

Living from the middle has something to do with being able to see life's beginning and end. We have gathered to shower our daughters with aunty-wisdom—drinking tea and sips of wine as we prepare a young woman for marriage—and to celebrate birthdays with friends who are living with diseases known to take lives. We have lived long enough to understand the meaning and value of wandering, and we live the lesson of needing to explore the world without forgetting who we were in the beginning. Each of us has danced the movements of *auana* and wandered far from the home place, where a backyard sock-baseball diamond was a giants' field, requiring many strides to reach second base.

Some days pass like racing clouds in front of a nearly full moon. The shape and luster of the clouds shift without asking, and delight pairs of human eyes as we watch how quickly the skyscape changes. Seated on the smooth caramel-colored slats of the worn teak bench, a childhood companion joins me in the sharing of one of those times, when clouds race, and moonbeams play. Forty years earlier, this friend and I spent time in this same backyard, and played in the shadows of the trees. In the shade of mango boughs, we spent time together in places bound in the magic syrup of children's imaginations. We did things without organization. Our parents didn't watch; they left us to our world. In the process, memories were created to be shared again and again in seamless film between *keìa* and *kela*. *Keìa*, now. *Kela*, over there.

Five years ago I returned to Kuliòuòu Valley on the island of Oàhu. More than twenty years away from the homeplace had changed me. I had adapted to life in a small, white, middle-class community in Washington State. Through the years, I chose to tuck my Hawaiian spirit tightly away in a *puòlo* bundle, and only shared it sparingly. To be "myself" out loud would have been too much. Instead, I bottled up most of the longings for home, and grafted a new form of being onto my original stock of twenty-four-year-old growth. On the outside, I learned to wear layers of long underwear to keep me warm. Although we raised our son along the shores of beautiful Puget Sound, I can count on two hands the number of times I swam in this nearly salty, rarely warm water. My body allowed layers of silk, polyester and cotton to surround me when the cool days of fall turned to winter cold. But this woman of warm Pacific saltwater never forgot the feel of Waimanalo Beach water—the temperature of my mother's womb, the texture and enveloping comfort unmatched. It was this water and the wind *ka makani* that always called.

Divorce poked *puka*, holes, in that *puòlo*, and my spirit began to flow from the tightly bound container. It was a messy sight, that ooze. My mother raised me to be loyal. Ma's steadfast jaw and lifelong mantra "never change horses in midstream" became part of my condition. Genetics gave me the jaw. The mantra was an old melody I lived without questioning, until Roy told me he wanted a divorce. I still hear our son Christopher telling us, "I can accept that, but it will take time for me to understand it." Ahhh. The tall, lacy fingers of cedar soothed me as healing salves do, and slowly allowed me to begin re-dreaming myself, gathering up my oozing spirit into something yet to be. The wind inside me knew it was time to go home and make peace with the *puka* and move with my spirit flow. *Ka Makani*—the wind outside—reminded me that a journey of migration meanders, and her movements carry no judgment.

When a woman remakes herself, as she must do many times while in the body, the skills of navigating and translating are called upon without thinking. If we are to move with the water, as people of the canoe, we must be able to read the way. Signs, shifts, and nature's messages are often subtle, and translating them accurately takes practice. Living as island people on a postage-stamp piece of earth surrounded by ocean is humbling. There is a balance and a promise that is our birthright. Live only on the white part of the stamp, on the edges. *Malama*, care for, the middle, because the land will continue to feed you. Forget that, and the stamp shrinks.

Ka Makani, the shape-shifting wind, blew me home. The moments, minutes, days and weeks of being back where I began have allowed me to experience what Natalie Goldberg calls "wild mind." The *puka* made by divorce are no longer the enemy. They are instead tiny portals pecked in my grafted self at forty-six, as escape hatches, openings to this wild mind. Without them, my spirit might have remained contained, root-bound, restless and fermenting. In the culture of my mother's people, they would say I was finally *Nana I Ke Kumu,* looking to the source.

The people of old say that the wind carries with her everything and everybody that ever was, and stirs with it all that is now—on the way to becoming everything that might be. Nature has always been a broad mirror that island people view without having to look. This morning the wind is gentle, but strong enough to send the bamboo-anchored paper screens into their click-clank, click-clank wind dance against the front window. The yama bells dangling outside are quiet. I wake before the sun brightens Kuliòuòu's dark sides from a deep and delicious night of sleep. Pete stirs beside me and I remember it is Monday morning. A travel day.

Sweethearts and friendships at fifty-two include expanded definitions for being. My long and lanky partner and companion works with his brother on Maui. The two men are creating a welding and metal-fabricating shop in Kahului, the Maui town where airplanes land and take off like the commuter ferries in Washington, loaded with folks who live in one place and work in another. The style of living that includes commuter relationships is one born from my time of shape shifting. This two-island kind of life gives me more time to know who I am alone.

Being alone without being lonely is a different thing for me. No marriage. No children. No job. The absence of all three has meant getting to know what and who I am before I relate to a partner, a child, or society's expectations. Coming home to hear myself means being courageous. It's not so much about being strong or moving fast anymore. I know I can be strong when I must, and accept that I'd rather not move quite as fast as I used to. I know the route, remember the clamber. Being courageous means being committed and prepared to be alone sometimes. At this point, I have made peace with the *puka*, the holes within me, and have replaced strength and speed with discernment and progress. Believing that "simple" works has meant accepting and celebrating my choices.

My parents created a life for me that worked during the years when familiar faces shared gentle, regular conversations, and yards were without squeeching gates and head-high fences. There are times now when the sounds of gas-powered chainsaws, leaf-blowers, lawn-mowers, and weed-whackers raise the decibel levels to a chaotic frenzy, torturing my ears and nervous system. So, I push my reel mower and feel a small but smiling voice inside saying, "Yah." While doing my taxes, my accountant says, "You are in the lowest income bracket. It takes courage to do that." I look across his boomerang-shaped table and nod. "Life is short," is all I say.

One of the decisions I made at fifty was to invest in myself now. My retirement funds, chocked away years ago when I worked full-time and at full speed, are a major source of income for me now. The simplified living I practice from this Kuliòuòu Valley home place, one day at a time, is simple but not always easy.

The hedges of mock orange that are everywhere in this valley are potent and pollen-packed. They send bees into a stupor, and folks like me, with allergies to their fragrance, into temporary refuge. After many years away from these hedges, I have learned that too much of a sweet thing can be just that. Too much! It's part of that discernment training that a *makua oò*, a maturing adult, must commit to as the body becomes less young, and as the systems within the *kino* lose their capacity to resist assault from pollens, free radicals, or aging attitudes like "controlling the world." It's funny how a hedgeful of tiny blossoms stimulates a new set of capacities for survival. Slowly, strength builds from the inside, and a life I stitch together moment to moment becomes new skin. Gratitude for small miracles and the grace to accept the perfection of an imperfect world fill the *puka* of a once-rigid view of how to be. My bank account breathes because there is so much space there. Open to the potential of "wild mind," I write because that's what I love. These years lived from the middle require more rest, and a gentle but courageous commitment to be a mountain, as I train to be a yoga teacher at fifty-two, and drink tea instead of a soda.

It matters less that others agree with me than it matters that I choose. Slowly—because that's the way nature works, slow to medium—I remember that my birthright is to live on the edge of the postage stamp, and to *malama*, care, for the middle. I choose to be a *Makuahine oò*, a maturing adult woman living gently on the earth, paying loving attention to the details of nature in the belief that I am part of a grander plan. *Nana I Ke Kumu.* I look to the Source.

The Calling

JOANNE B. MULCAHY

You would know when *the call* came. Father McGuire stood in front
of the class, ample body swaying side to side, brow knit in concentration. His hand covered his heart, then touched his ear. "You'll have
to listen hard, inside and out." I focused on the white hairs edging
Father's ears, on the blue eyes shining in his craggy face. A shiver
snaked through my body. Mystery surrounded the summons to
a vocation: How would you recognize your calling? Some knowledge cannot be stated, only pointed to. A vocation yoked some inner
awareness to an outer path, an umbilicus that sought growth rather
than severance. Like much in Catholicism, this truth rested on paradox: a calling couldn't be directly pursued. But honoring the mysteries, serving others, and performing the proper rituals could nudge
you toward spiritual readiness.

Father McGuire and the other priests who visited our classes
at St. Ursula's surely meant the convent or rectory as the place to
which one is called. But I didn't think of vocation as strictly religious.
Ambiguity can be a blessing. I shaped my life around a secret yearning for *the call*. It would arrive on the wings of ritual, so I said my
prayers three times daily. I lit candles in church and on the advent
wreath before Christmas. I followed the Stations of the Cross during
Lent, relinquished half my candy to anonymous orphans on All

Saints' Day, and proudly displayed my darkened forehead on Ash Wednesday. I was waiting to be called.

And then I wasn't. By age thirteen, I longed to shed the trappings of Irish-Catholicism. To expel the voices that echoed in my head en route to school: *Be modest in thought, word, and deed. Serve others in God's name.* I was the second of six children, the one who gave up the extra pork chop at dinner, the one to whom others told their problems, the one who accompanied my mother when she carried a Pyrex pan of tuna casserole to sickly Mrs. O'Connor. One year, my parents made a Christmas card in the form of a coloring book. About me they wrote, "Color her martyr-like."

With adolescence came babysitting on Saturday nights, illuminating a non-Catholic world. My favorite family was the Boras, who had an only child named Billy. His oneness stunned me—a sapling standing apart from a distant forest. Mr. Bora paid me with bills unfurled from a thick wad in his pocket, always supplementing the standard fifty cents per hour. I loved sinking into the Boras' stark white wraparound couch, worlds away from the sagging daybed in our square, brick house. We had books at home; my parents believed in education and Catholicism with nearly equal zeal. Some knowledge could be sought, and once held, it was yours, a bundle to clutch like the sequined bag my mother carried on rare Saturday nights out. While our shelves were filled with dictionaries, *Reader's Digest Condensed Books,* and Nancy Drew mysteries, the Boras' held *Othello* and *As I Lay Dying.* Here lay seeds whose growth would extend into new domains. A magazine called *Avant Garde* graced their coffee table. Little matter that the words meant nothing to me; the pages reeked of cosmopolitan chic, of a secular world beyond the boundaries of St. Ursula's.

A transfer from Catholic to public school deepened my yearning. Dismissed was the clannish "blood is thicker than water" dictum of my large family; I would be singular. Gone was the passive surrender of the martyr to God or destiny; I would serve myself. The seductive scent of self-definition banished incense; learning replaced mystery. Escape was imminent, my destination the cool, crisp certainty of the intellectual.

What does knowledge mean? Perception and identification, says the *Oxford English Dictionary,* but also "recognition." When a writer articulates some truth we can't yet state, we literally quiver with what we almost already know. Or so says the journal I kept as a teenager. Aldous Huxley speaks of perception's doors cleansed; Fyodor Dostoevsky of compassion; Joan Didion of self-respect; and Virginia Woolf of professions for women. But searing at the center of the notebook's yellowing pages is a caveat from Andre Gide's *Oedipus;* there are people, he cautions, who pursue in books the "authority to bore, oppress and terrorize their neighbors."

At sixteen, I must have written these words with a shaky hand. Wrong intention could block one's path. If books were my chosen gods, how would I avoid such minefields? Nearing fifty, now a teacher for fifteen years, I quake still. What do I seek in knowledge? Have I realized my path, and how might I guide students toward theirs?

Between those bookended hopes and fears, a circuitous unfolding.

My high school years fade in the hazy memory of the smoking rooms at Haverford College library near our house outside Philadelphia. I skipped school to spend days there lounging in a red leather chair, Russian novels and Marlboros my companions. The month before graduation found me running the track and hanging from rings to make up the required number of gym classes. The striped uniform seemed fitting attire for my final weeks of high school imprisonment.

During my last year at the University of Pennsylvania, I frequently revisited the red leather chair in that same smoking room to study Russian. My route there had snaked back and forth between waitress jobs and through three different colleges, the institutions always secondary to the libraries. The thick-tongued pleasure of reciting Cyrillic words, the expansive hours perusing dictionaries—the rituals of learning marked me like invisible tattoos. I believed that they would surround me with a magic cloak and transport me to the day when I awoke simply knowing my path.

I found fellow travelers in surprising corners. In 1979, I moved to Kodiak Island, Alaska, to join my boyfriend, Bill. Our fishing community brimmed with educational iconoclasts: a high school dropout who quoted Nietzsche, a multilingual Norwegian with little formal schooling who taught us to make salmon sausage, and a biologist who introduced me to magical realism. Dozens of transients passed through our bungalow overlooking the boat harbor. Fire, a flame-haired, self-taught chiropractor lived in our front room for months. Clients never questioned his lack of medical training; in Alaska, knowledge often cleaved from institutional education. Radical egalitarianism was the ethos. If you had a Harvard degree—and some fishermen did—you didn't flaunt it. Besides, book learning wouldn't save you from the Gulf of Alaska's frigid waters.

On Kodiak, my rituals changed. By day, I waited tables, pickled herring, and wrote in my journal, shaping experience in my black and white copybook. At night, I answered crisis calls for the women's resource center. Some of our clients fleeing violence came from the six Native Alutiiq villages ringing Kodiak's outer edges. One night, a call alerted us that a woman named Mary Peterson was flying in from Akhiok, a windswept community of a hundred people. As

salmon fishing and cannery work slackened, booze runs had in-
creased. Guns meant to bring home venison came out after family
arguments. Mary sometimes slept under the house to escape her
husband when he drank. When we met at the airport, her youthful appearance shocked me. She was calm, assured, seemingly un-
scathed by years of hardship.

I went on to interview Mary and nearly thirty other Alutiiq
women about village life. Central to their stories was the midwife, a
heroic figure who saved women from Western medicine's perceived
indifference. Of Mary's eighteen children, only those born in the
hospital died. "All my children that lived were delivered by midwives. In the hospital, they didn't care enough to make them live,
didn't stay with the baby all night like the midwives did." Western
medical practice overshadowed, then outlawed Native healing; by
mid-twentieth century, women delivered in hospitals. History books
told this story; quietly subversive, Alutiiq women told another, holding firm to their belief in the superiority of Native methods.

Few elders had gone past the elementary grades in village
schools, yet their knowledge was vast, oral, and rooted in tradition.
Mary Peterson described becoming a midwife: "I always wanted to
help. The first time with a baby, I just *knew*, like I'd been doing it a
long time, like God was guiding my hands." She trusted her path,
just as she did that the salmon would run in the Red River and the
first salmonberries bud on the hills above Akhiok each year.

What did it mean to apprehend the world in this way? Did Mary
feel a shiver of prescience before knowledge arrived? Listening to
her stories, I hovered on the brink of my childhood: the mystery of
almost knowing, finding meaning in serving others, waiting for a
summons.

I'd come to Alaska intoxicated with freedom and in control of my destiny. I suspected that Mary and the other women I met on Kodiak regarded me—unmarried, childless, unmoored, and always questioning—with puzzlement and perhaps pity. Was I the person they saw, or the one I was creating?

⁓

My hands slid from the computer keys on a clammy August night in Washington, D.C. For months, I'd been tethered to my computer writing a dissertation on Alutiiq women's stories. I rose at 6 a.m. to write, worked afternoons at the Smithsonian Institution, and then waited tables for a caterer. My life was scheduled, controlled, driven toward completing a PhD. For a decade, I'd studied linguistics, anthropology, literary theory, folklore, and feminism. I could talk about postmodernism, deconstruction, and sociolinguistics. What I wanted to talk about was hiking up Pillar Mountain on a Kodiak August night, the glint of fireweed on the hillside. But dissertation writing is not storytelling; theory has little use for sensuous detail.

I'd gone to graduate school in passionate pursuit of knowledge, seduced by the Boras' avant-garde and the sheer pleasure of learning. But Gide's warnings revived. At lunch tables, other students held forth on works of social theory, prefacing remarks with "Surely you've read...." Usually, I hadn't. I studied constantly, but now it seemed that I'd never accumulate enough. Debates focused on scholarships and dissertation topics best suited for the job market. The wonder I felt in the Haverford College smoking rooms began to fade. One afternoon, I fled a lecture to sob uncontrollably in a narrow bathroom stall. My body felt denied, my connections to others severed, my status as an imposter confirmed. I'd never find my path.

Depression so severe that I couldn't rise in the morning finally sent me to a counselor. "You'll get over it," said Deb, a student-counselor not much older than me, "this questioning of what knowledge is for and where you belong. You'll finish here, get a job, and move on. It's part of the individuation process."

After years of struggling for singularity, I was stunned to discover that I didn't want to individuate. Professional life dangled like a skeleton in the gaping void. Drowning in books and theory, I craved a return to mystery, a connection to something larger than myself.

Writing my dissertation in Washington, D.C., I sensed the old gnawing hunger. Beyond the window, night thickened with swarming mosquitoes and the Potomac River's dank scent. Strolling couples' laughter hung viscous in the air. My writing mimicked the humidity—slow, plodding, stuck-in-the-head. I turned back to the chapter I'd begun—the story of meeting Mary Peterson on Kodiak. As I closed my eyes, memories rushed back: gleaming snow on Barometer Mountain, long nights spent writing in my journal, then an event that occurred just weeks after I'd met Mary. A woman called one night from a trailer park; before details emerged, someone cut the phone line. Intuition made me think the caller was Mary. I ignored a central rule of the women's center: never go to a crisis scene. Dense fog settled as I steered the pickup around Dead Man's Curve toward the trailer park. Heart pounding, I crept among the oblong shapes, searching in the thick mist. What was I after that night? What was I searching for at age twenty-four, far from home, drawn to the moral certainty of a woman who knew who she was and what her life was for?

I never found Mary Peterson in the trailer park; we would reconnect years later. But recovering the memory on that humid night in Washington, D.C., I discovered something else. Entering Mary's world, defying the academic rules, I wrote with my body, or through it, released from control. The chapter finished as though it wrote itself. For those hours that felt like an extended moment, I *knew* something.

Maybe Mary felt such knowing all the time, or perhaps only when her hands soothed a suffering body or eased a woman's labor. I would never fathom what she knew, the chasm of cultural difference stubborn between us. But now there was this—the experience of ecstatic release. I sat in my apartment, silent, sweating, rapt, sensing something at the boundaries of body and spirit and mind. I felt small and insignificant, huge and powerful.

Becoming a teacher was an accident. Yearning for Alaska, I ventured west again, landing in Oregon. Funding for my job directing an arts program fell through. In a panic, I took an adjunct position, stunned by how immediately I loved teaching. Still, old fears hovered: Did I really know enough?

After a decade of teaching, my partner, Bob, and I led an overseas trip to Australia. With seventeen students, we attended lectures, camped in the outback, snorkeled on the Great Barrier Reef, and lived with Aboriginal people. The students got sick, fell in love, and blundered as we all do in other cultures. I woke one day grateful to find that I knew them as full human beings.

Returning to Portland, my first class was a seminar in feminist theory. Many young women in my gender studies classes voiced frustration with theory. Why did the language so often tangle into an indecipherable thicket? Sometimes I shared their feelings; still, I couldn't abandon the pleasure of untangling the web. I wanted students to embrace that challenge too, prodding them to read French psychoanalysis and challenges to Marx and Freud. But after Australia, something shifted. I stood before the class and acknowledged the plea in their eyes: tell us why we should study this. My tongue swelled with doublespeak: because theory is a crystalline tool to pry open the mind; because mastery will protect you from Gide's terrorizing minions; but above all, because I want you to believe that a

Catholic girl can transcend her parochial upbringing, move beyond the embarrassing emotionality of belief, fight the yearning for mystery, and despite barely graduating from high school, might finally *know* something.

I jettisoned the syllabus after the first week. We started reading poetry and memoir as well as theory, writing personal essays in addition to critical papers. I stopped giving grades. Students had to find something more compelling than my judgment to motivate them, something raw inside that drew them outward. Each day in class, Father McGuire hovered in the shadows, hand touching his heart, then his ear, urging our listening.

I hold fast to Father's image and the shimmering possibility a vocation evoked in me. I feel called to nurture others as a teacher, a beckoning to service not dissimilar from the old dictums of Church and family that I tried so hard to escape. I feel called when students strain to grasp theory, learning to savor its rewards. I feel called, too, when they discover their own path through writing, linking something internal to an outer world. I feel called to tell the stories of Mary Peterson and other women who invited my imagination beyond the boundaries of Western culture, enabling a burst of faith as well as intellectual struggle.

What is knowledge for? I queried at sixteen, certain that the answer would emerge when I'd amassed enough. But teaching taught me otherwise. What we know isn't containable, a bundle to be grasped, but the wellspring that mysteriously replenishes as we give it away. Teaching proved as magical and mysterious as a fairy tale and as rigorous as a geometric theorem, an alchemy of heart and mind and spirit. The nuns and priests at St. Ursula's taught me well about accepting such paradox. But my greatest teacher has been the writing process. In trusting each day that words will come, I honor the same grace within myself that I nurture in others. Writing pushes us inward and outward simultaneously, yielding to what we seek but cannot ask for.

Each morning before I sit down to write, I open a bottle of holy water I brought home from the Lough Derg pilgrimage in County Donegal, Ireland. Into a tiny Mexican ceramic bowl mounted on my wall, I pour a few drops. Dipping my hand in the water, I feel again the power of childhood rituals, of being humbled by life's mysteries. I used to think such surrender equaled a denial of the individual. I now see it as an expansion of the self, prelude to discovering a path both singular and deeply connected.

Mopping the Floor

CHINA GALLAND

The beauty of youth is like a flash of
lightning in the sky and wealth is unstable
like dew on the tip of a blade of grass.

Friends and relatives are inconstant
like customers at the market place.

Bestow your blessings so that I may be able to
understand the true nature of impermanence.

PRAYERS OF REQUEST TO THE LADY TARA

(TRANSLATED BY CAROL SAVVAS)

MOTHER TERESA'S HOME FOR
THE ELDERLY, KATHMANDU

Tibetan drums announce the beginning of the day in Boudha. The
drone of chanting swells the air, forming a cushion around the
dog barks and blare of horns from nearby streets. Raucous crows
call from the veranda. Federica and I are going to work at Mother
Teresa's Home for the Elderly in Pashupatinath this morning.
Mother Teresa is a well-known example of this fierce, no-nonsense,
protective spirit that I seek. I remember an early story I heard of how

Mother Teresa, when she first went out into the streets of Calcutta to begin her ministry, picked up a dying woman, took her to the hospital, and refused to leave until the woman was cared for. Her commitment to compassion for the poor and the cast-out is fierce. However, I am interested in her Sisters, in the Missionaries of Charity, the little-known women in the background who, day after day, are carrying out Mother Teresa's ministry. What are they like? I'm sure that her Sisters will show me another face of the compassionate fierce feminine. The bond between Mother Teresa and her Sisters is legendary, and the strength of it forms the basis of the success of her order. Mother Teresa might have been a wonder, but without her Sisters, her work would not be the internationally recognized phenomenon that it's become. This is why I want to be with her Sisters. Though they may be quiet nuns, they would have to have a kind of fierceness in them to face the suffering that they do, day after day. And I'm apprehensive, grateful that Federica's coming with me.

I heat up rice and *dahl* for breakfast, prepare to make a cup of tea. Getting ready for the day, even just making a cup of tea, requires a kind of thought that I'm not used to as a Westerner. In the back of my mind as I bustle around the kitchen, putting on the water to boil, I wonder if I'm being initiated into our future as water pollution and shortages continue. I stop myself, remembering suddenly that I have to turn on the electric water pump.

The water supply in Kathmandu has been drained so low that water is pumped into the system only once or twice a day. Everyone tries to draw water during the few hours it's available, creating an even greater shortage. Sometimes there is no water whatsoever, like in the small, elegantly crumbling former palace where I first stayed, in a friend's apartment. There we pumped drinking water by hand every morning. In order to prevent dysentery and the other waterborne diseases so common here, one boils the water for twenty minutes, cools it, then pours it through a charcoal filtering system. Any

Nepali home that can afford it uses this filter system in addition to boiling the water. Living in one of the poorest countries in the world, most Nepalis cannot. Water-borne diseases plague the populace, putting millions of lives at risk every year, especially those of women and children. At home, where I am blessed to be able to drink water out of the tap, the reality of the loss of clean water barely penetrates. Here, where the limits of clean water have been breached so severely, the madness of this is unavoidable.

The third-floor flat I've rented at Boudha is equipped with not only the manual filtering system but also an electric pump, a luxury here. If I remember to turn on the pump and the neighbors aren't using theirs at the same time, there is water in the tap, water to boil and filter, a process that takes roughly two hours. One has to think ahead, prepare beforehand. No going into the kitchen in the middle of the night to get a drink of water out of the tap.

Even the cup holding the tea made from boiled and filtered water is not to be taken for granted, my host explained, for dishes are washed with tap water. Cups, dishes, silverware, everything at least has to have boiled water poured over it and then be dried off. Having nearly died of amoebic dysentery from the water here before, I take all precautions.

There'll be no bathing this morning, as not only does the water pump have to be turned on for ten minutes to fill the hot-water heater, the water also has to be heated, and that takes at least two hours. The hot-water tank takes so much electricity, very expensive here, that it is turned on only two hours beforehand. Tonight, I tell myself, I'll bathe tonight, as I turn down the propane fire under the rice and *dahl*. The propane tank is low. Forget the stove. Time to go! I have to meet Federica at the north end of the stupa.

⁓

Mother Teresa's Sisters maintain the only home for the elderly in the entire country of Nepal, in one wing of Pashupatinath, the most

revered Hindu temple complex in the country. Situated on the Bag-
mati River, Pashupati is known for its burning *ghats*, steps into the
river, and the platforms just above them, where devout Hindus are
cremated in the open on crackling funeral pyres, as on the Ganges
in India. After meeting Aruna, Agnes, and later Olga Murray, who
works with street children and orphans, sometimes rescuing them
from jail, where they may be confined with their mothers, I view the
clamoring street children who swarm around me now differently.

I visited Olga and many former street children at J House, one of
the orphanages Olga started with her colleague Allen Ailstrop. An
attorney in her seventies, retired from more than thirty years with
the California State Supreme Court, Olga started the Nepalese
Youth Opportunity Foundation (NYOF) to educate and provide
for as many of these street children as possible. I met Devi-Maya,
a blind girl who at five had her arm broken in three places by a
drunken father so that she would be a more effective beggar. Devi-
Maya now lives happily at J House and is the first in her class at
the school for the blind. I met Ganu, a little girl who had been badly
burned but who also advanced rapidly in school and could now
dance, thanks to the medical care NYOF provided. Without Olga's
passion for these children, hundreds would have been left on the
street with no way to receive an education or the medical care many
need. A great many would have been lost, kidnapped, stolen, sold
into debt bondage or prostitution.

Street children are especially vulnerable to the dangers of child
trafficking. When Federica and I climb out of the taxi they rush us. It
is hard simply to be with what I now know about the life of these
children. There are so many of them, at least fifteen around us now,
that it is clear that I can do nothing, at least not in this moment, not
by myself. My respect for these women for taking on the problems
they have grows each day.

Federica and I refuse all the children. I shake my head, no, I don't want to buy jewelry, I say to one; no, I don't want to see burning bodies today, to another, who wants to walk me to the *ghats* to view a cremation. No. Federica and I duck through an open gateway into the temple complex to find the Sisters.

The main building at Pashupati is a large rectangular structure around a large open courtyard filled with small shrines. Mother Teresa's Sisters have a wing to themselves for the elderly. A tall, broad-shouldered woman named Sister Edwin greets Federica and me as we walk in. Wiping her hands across her blue-and-white-checked apron before she extends them, Sister Edwin is a large woman, substantial, cheerful, and efficient. There is little wasted time or motion around Sister Edwin. There's another volunteer here this morning, a young woman from Denmark who's spending three months working with the Sisters.

"We're mopping the floors, and they need drying. The section on the right has been done. Dry that first," Sister Edwin says to me, handing me a small clean towel. She tells Federica to help the other woman finish mopping the long room on our left. Drying a wet cement floor with one small towel? It's not much bigger than a washcloth. I'm not sure how this can be done, much less how helpful it is. I do it anyway. An old man sits cross-legged on the bed next to the one under which I'm drying. He's weak and cold and struggling to pull a shawl around his shoulders. I dry my hands on my skirt and stand up to help him. He must be in his nineties. He could have been my grandfather, I think as I bend over, pulling the shawl up around his shoulders. No, he wants it over his head too, he lets me know.

Sister Raissa comes along and pours warm milk into the cup he holds out. I kneel back down to continue drying under the bed. Suddenly I'm being splattered with warm milk. It's the old man sprinkling me. He does it again while I'm looking right at him. His eyes twinkle and he laughs, pleased at the surprise on my face. Just what he wanted. I am flooded with inexplicable delight.

Looking up past the old man, I see on the wall a well-known saying from Mother Teresa, "Christ needs our hands, our eyes, our hearts. . . ." It reminds me of what a Tibetan lama said when he first visited the Benedictine shrine of the Black Madonna at Einsiedeln, in Switzerland. Yes, the Madonna was very beautiful and her temple impressive, he thought, but he was more curious about what the people who were devoted to her were like. The divine feminine needs our hands, our eyes, our hearts too. Mary, Christ's mother, is the Western counterpart of Tara, the Mother of All the Buddhas, that's why he had been taken to see her shrine.

"It's the practitioner who brings the deity through," the lama explained. It's through the practitioner, the one who is devoted to her, that the power of the Madonna will show herself. The beaten gold backdrop of her altar, the drawers full of jewels given to her, her exquisitely embroidered robes, the ex-votos in the back of the church —paintings of the miracles she had performed, visual thank-you notes—the importance of the centuries-old Benedictine monastery that housed the shrine were undoubtedly noteworthy and impressive, this Tibetan monk thought, but what were her devotees like? Had she tamed their minds and hearts, helped rid them of destructive impulses, made them more generous, more compassionate, more loving, as followers of Tara are taught in Tibetan Buddhism? This is what he wanted to know. Had she destroyed the demons of greed, hate, and delusion in her followers, like Durga and Kali, had she pierced their hearts, could she save the world?

As I continue drying the floor I think about Mother Teresa and the Sisters working here, and I encounter a paradox. What we imagine about God, Tara, the Buddha, Jesus, Durga—whatever or whomever it is we might call the divine—can be made up only of what we have seen people doing as they live out their lives. What

Gandhi, Martin Luther King, Jr., Harriet Tubman, Dorothy Day, Mother Henriette Delille, the Dalai Lama, and countless others did and do is where my ideas of compassion, charity, patience, wisdom, love, and generosity come from, not from any text or teaching. Henriette Delille was a nineteenth-century New Orleans free woman of color who founded the Sisters of the Holy Family, an African-American order of Sisters, in 1843, during a time when African-American women were not allowed to be nuns and people could be put to death for teaching people in slavery to read. Henriette taught anyway. She fed and educated the poorest of the poor, the children, the old slaves, the discarded. I think of her now because she was an early Mother Teresa, too little known, though her Sisters are promoting her cause for canonization as a saint. Mother Henriette's life inspires me time and time again. She will be the first African-American woman saint, when and if she is canonized.

The floors here are washed every morning and swabbed down with disinfectant. This long room of beds doubles as an open hospital ward. I am drying the floor so that no one will slip and fall. A woman in the section Federica mopped had terrible open bedsores when she was brought in a few weeks ago. Sister Edwin is cleaning one just as I finish the floor and go to find her for further instructions.

I wince as Sister Edwin cleans. Sister Raissa sees me and says cheerfully in her British clip, "Oh, this is much better. She is really healing. When she first came, this sore was ten inches across and you could see the bone." The woman moans softly as Sister Edwin deftly and quickly swabs it with sterile cotton soaked with disinfectant. I gasp under my breath. The woman's husband stands at her feet, looking gently at his wife, who is quietly bearing her pain and the curiosity of the day's volunteers. They have four children and are very poor. He comes to feed her three times a day.

Nepali radio blares, horns honk, and a sitar drones in the background. Suddenly a group of tourists walks into the infirmary and begins taking photographs, even though there are signs that say clearly "No Pictures." I walk up to them and inquire if they read English, pointing to the sign. They apologize, in English, and retreat, snapping more pictures as they move backward out the doorway. Sister Edwin finishes up with her patient.

"Outside!" she announces. "It's ladies' bathing day. Please come and help," she says as she turns toward the courtyard, and signals to an old man to fetch more water for warming. Federica and I follow.

We move outside to an aging green hand pump as the old women gather for their weekly bathing. The sky is clear and sunny this morning, no smog. The air is mild. The Sisters pumped water earlier this morning and heated it in big tubs now set out on the courtyard stones. Sister Edwin hands me a cup and a bar of soap, throws a towel over my shoulder matter-of-factly, and says, "Like this," as she begins to chat and vigorously soap up a partially dressed old woman. With quick, sure movements, always careful to preserve the woman's modesty, she washes and rinses her in no time and moves on to the next woman.

The women wear saris even as they are being bathed. The woman Sister Edwin bathes moves deftly out of her dirty clothes, simultaneously wrapping herself with swift movements that leave no private part exposed. No matter how old and arthritic the person, each maintains a remarkable dignity. Sister Edwin motions me over to a blind woman she wants me to bathe. My charge suddenly squats down a few feet away and begins to urinate.

"Sister, Sister, what do I do?" I ask, flustered, as my first assignee sits urinating all over her feet.

Sister Edwin laughs and dips her large cup into one of the tubs of water and swishes the urine away. "Nothing to do." She giggles, and says in her clipped English, "She must be out of those clothes anyway. Help her finish undressing and throw them in the laundry pile.

They'll all get washed and boiled tomorrow. Everyone gets fresh clothes once a week with their bath. No harm."

"Sister, you wash all those clothes by hand?" I ask after seeing the growing size of the already three-foot-high pile of washing in the little laundry hut in the courtyard.

"Prayer makes everything easy, if we are doing it for God," Sister Edwin assures me. She has been a nun for twenty-two years. "All this that we are doing here at Mother Teresa's—all over the world— Mother started with only five rupees. That is all. She just started teaching the children. The first school was so poor that she had to draw the letters on the dirt floor.

"Five rupees. That's how she started. Doing it for God."

The blind woman stands up now, relieved. She must be four feet ten. Like all the women here, her head has been shorn, for lice, for ease of care, I don't know which. Her eyes are half closed in her blindness, but she smiles as I begin to pour warm water over her. She turns her face up like a flower to the warmth of the sun and stream- ing water, clearly enjoying it. Gently I soap her bare shoulders, her arms, and then reach down the back of her sari as far as I can with my soapy cloth and warm water. Then I do the same with her front; this isn't half as terrifying or difficult as I imagined the moment it was announced that it was time to help with the bathing. This is not a person who cannot move or do anything for herself. Though old and blind, she is ambulatory and lively. Between the two of us, we get her respectably clean and well rinsed.

Next comes the drying, toweling her off and then pulling a rough cotton green-and-white-checked dress over her head as she lets her wet sari drop. Now she is bathed, clean, and dressed, her silvery head shining in the morning sunlight. I help her into a purple sweater as she lets me put first one arm then the other into the sleeves and then pull it up over her shoulders.

Marigolds bloom in the courtyard. An old man comes out to

help with the hand pump, for the Sisters need more water. A young retarded man with a limp, wearing a bright green turban, teeters past on his uneven legs, his empty tin plate in his hands, ready for lunch to be served.

"We can't serve food to the elderly because we are low caste," Sister Edwin explains with a hearty laugh. "We are not Brahmin. Brahmins can only be served by Brahmins. They won't take food from our hands even if they're hungry. Yours either. Brahmin volunteers come in to serve them."

"Sister," I call back to her, now bathing her third charge in the time it took me to wash this one, "what is this woman's name?"

"Oh, that's Tara," she says, as the old blind woman smiles at me in the sunlight.

"Tara?" I repeat, taken aback.

"Yes," Sister says as she briskly towels off another woman. Federica laughs as she overhears our interchange. I had told her about my trip to Pharping to measure the Tara with Christina. She looks up and gives me a broad grin, raising her eyebrows and nodding her head knowingly, "Tara, eh-h?" then goes back to carefully trimming the toenails of the old woman she has just finished bathing.

I accompany this Tara with chipped pink fingernails to a place where she can sit down and enjoy the warmth of the morning sun, and then I begin to bathe the next woman Sister Edwin points out.

I have to laugh out loud as I think to myself, So this is it. Tara *is* growing, maybe not in the rock at Pharping but in the form of the joyful old blind woman who stands before me. This old Tara is a complete renunciate. Whether by intention or not, she has given up worldly possessions. She has only the one clean set of clothes she is given to wear weekly after her bath. She has only the food she is served, only the care she is given. She can initiate little or nothing by herself, and yet she seems quite happy. Did she always have simple wants and needs? I wonder as I turn and look at her again, sitting with her face turned toward the sun. Or could she have once known luxury and lost everything? Had she known the warmth of a family or had she always been alone?

What a teaching on acceptance this living Tara is giving me. Perhaps we have no more choices about our situation than this woman, only we labor under illusions that old age strips away so starkly here. We are dependent, deeply dependent upon the kindness of one another and the bonds between us.

Finding myself bathing Tara is a sweet consolation. I've always thought that the story of Tara growing out of the rock was a metaphor. Finding this Tara at Mother Teresa's confirms that intuition. She reveals herself through service, not only devotion. Mother Teresa's Sisters and this aging Tara remind me that the divine manifests itself in the person in front of me and that service can help me see that.

The Measure of My Days

FLORIDA SCOTT-MAXWELL

A mother's love for her children, even her inability to let them be, is because she is under a painful law that the life that passed through her must be brought to fruition. Even when she swallows it whole she is only acting like any frightened mother cat eating its young to keep it safe. It is not easy to give closeness and freedom, safety plus danger.

No matter how old a mother is, she watches her middle-aged children for signs of improvement. It could not be otherwise for she is impelled to know that the seeds of value sown in her have been winnowed. She never outgrows the burden of love, and to the end she carries the weight of hope for those she bore. Oddly, very oddly, she is forever surprised and even faintly wronged that her sons and daughters are just people, for many mothers hope and half expect that their new-born child will make the world better, will somehow be a redeemer. Perhaps they are right, and they can believe that the rare quality they glimpsed in the child is active in the burdened adult.

How understandable that most of our beliefs protect us from the danger of being an individual. "Think of others," we were once taught. "Adapt, adapt," we are now told. But it is a coward cry, for he who after cruel buffeting wins to aloneness learns that life is a tragic mystery. We are pierced and driven by laws we only half understand, we find that the lesson we learn again and again is that of accepting heroic helplessness. Some uncomprehended law holds us at a point of contradiction where we have no choice, where we do not like that which we love, where good and bad are inseparable partners impossible to tell apart, and where we—heartbroken and ecstatic, can only resolve the conflict by blindly taking it into our hearts. This used to be called being in the hands of God. Has anyone any better words to describe it?

Another secret we carry is that though drab outside—wreckage to the eye, mirrors a mortification—inside we flame with a wild life that is almost incommunicable. In silent, hot rebellion we cry silently—"I have lived my life haven't I? What more is expected of me?" Have we got to pretend out of noblesse oblige that age is nothing, in order to encourage the others? This we do with a certain haughtiness, realizing now that we have reached the place beyond resignation, a place I had no idea existed until I had arrived here.

It is a place of fierce energy. Perhaps passion would be a better word than energy, for the sad fact is this vivid life cannot be used. If I try to transpose it into action I am soon spent. It has to be accepted as passionate life, perhaps the life I never lived, never guessed I had it in me to live. It feels other and more than that. It feels like the far side of precept and aim. It is just life, the natural intensity of life, and when old we have it for our reward and undoing. It can—at moments—feel as though we had it for our glory. Some of it must go beyond good and bad, for at times—though this comes rarely, unexpectedly—it is a swelling clarity as though all was resolved. It has no content, it seems to expand us, it does not derive from the body, and then it is gone. It may be a degree of consciousness which lies outside activity, and which when young we are too busy to experience.

⁓

I often want to say to people, "You have neat, tight expectations of what life ought to give you, but you won't get it. That isn't what life does. Life does not accommodate you, it shatters you. It is meant to, and it couldn't do it better. Every seed destroys its container or else there would be no fruition."

But some wouldn't hear, and some would shatter themselves on principle.

⁓

My note book shows me how much I mourn. Perhaps the forms of life that are passing should be mourned, and this may be the right role of age. Perhaps our wail should be part of the paean of life that is being lived. I do not mourn for lost happiness, I do not mourn for myself. I mourn that life is so incomprehensible, and I mourn for this confused age. We old are the wailers. I hear us everywhere.

⁓

Easter Day

I am in that rare frame of mind when everything seems simple. When I have no doubt that the aim and solution of life is the acceptance of God. It is impossible and imperative, and clear. To open to such unimaginable greatness affrights my smallness. I do not know what I seek, cannot know, but I am where the mystery is the certainty.

My long life has hardly given me time—I cannot say to understand—but to be able to imagine that God speaks to me, says simply —"I keep calling to you, and you do not come," and I answer quite naturally—"I couldn't, until I knew there was nowhere else to go."

Wrestling with My Angel

MARILYN SEWELL

✒

*And Jacob was left alone; and there wrestled a man with him until the
breaking of the day.*
*And when he saw that he prevailed not against him, he touched the
hollow of his thigh; and the hollow of Jacob's thigh was out of
joint, as he wrestled with him.*
*And he said, Let me go, for the day breaketh. And he said, I will not let
thee go, except thou bless me.*

GENESIS 32:24–26

All my life I've been wrestling with my angel. Only recently, as I
enter my sixties, have I let go. I'm tired out from being angry at God.
I'm worn down with my own petty complaining. And I know beyond a doubt that there is no bargaining with the Holy One.

I thought the bargain I offered was an altogether reasonable one.
*I do your bidding, my God, and you send me love. I'll work hard harvesting in
your fields as a parish minister, and I'll earn affection, tenderness, care, and of
course passion, from a good man. It's all I ever wanted. Send the whole package,
please. Make it mutual, of course. Deal?*

We are made creatures of wanting, even as we first nuzzle for our
mother's milk. We *desire*. We want to be exempt from pain, disease,

accident, death. Especially death. It is disconcerting to discover that we are not special. We will suffer. We will die. *But before I die, let me love.*

Buddhist literature has led me to contemplate the dangers of this constant desire. Give up wanting? Give up my passion? It's a difficult notion for me. If a thing is good, give me more of it. By nature I am intense, eager, excessive, greedy, lustful. If life catches me in a no-win situation, I follow the advice of Mae West, who reportedly said, "If I'm forced to choose between two evils, I prefer to take the one I haven't tried yet."

My passion is more than a little tinged with anger, and it serves me well. If a wrong is to be set right, I'll stoke the fires of change with my fury, like some female Byronic hero. I cling fast to my outrage. Think twice before you go up against me. Think more than twice if you fancy loving me.

As a little six-year-old Catholic, I wanted a dog. So I prayed to the Virgin Mary for one, reminding her of my devotion to her Son and his Father, and a few weeks later I was rewarded by finding said dog, flea-ridden, sporting patches of pink mange on her thin tan coat, in the alley behind the filling station near my home. Her tail was curled between her legs, her ribs showing, her eyes turned down in fear. My parents didn't think too much of the Virgin's choice, but to me this dog was—well, the answer to my prayers. I named her Poochy, and I loved her and cared for her, and I knew that she loved me. On the day I stumbled upon her, I began to believe that petitionary prayer was the way to go, so long as I could be faithful to the rules and to the Maker of the Rules. So long as I could please my angel.

As I grew a bit older, I began to dream of a pony. At the age of eight, I could imagine nothing more fulfilling in my life than having a pony of my own. How envious the other children would be! How popular I would become! When my parents explained to me that ponies required pony sheds and pastures, and that we had neither, and that no pony would be forthcoming, I cried, complaining to the Virgin that life was indeed unfair. I vowed that when I became old enough to work, the first thing I would buy for myself would be a pony. I was a good girl. I would be rewarded. My dream was just postponed.

This weighty responsibility of constant virtue only grew heavier as events unfolded and the stakes became higher. Perhaps this would not have been so had my mother been with us as a ballast. But Daddy took us three children from her when I was nine, as she was sliding into a third nervous breakdown. We were living in Cincinnati at the time, her hometown, in a two-story white frame house on a tree-lined street. It was summer, and hot.

Big Papa and Uncle Gene drove up to our house one day in July. I didn't know they were coming. I was playing with my new puppy. Mother wasn't home. Daddy threw a sheet on the floor, pulled out drawers and dumped clothes inside, then tied the sheet up and threw it in the back end of Big Papa's Studebaker. We couldn't take my puppy, Daddy said. We could just take the clothes. Not my big bride doll, either. We all crowded into the car—Daddy and Big Papa and Donna and Jim and I—and Uncle Gene drove us fast, out of Cincinnati, into the countryside, across the river on a small railroad bridge with no rails, on across the state line to Kentucky, on toward Louisiana. I left a room of my own and my own bed with my shoes neatly tucked away. I left my box of "secrets" in its hiding place. I didn't see my mother again until I graduated from high school.

I can't remember Mother's face. Only six months, and her face is already lost. I am lying in bed beside my little sister, Donna, who is sleeping soundly. I hear the Frigidaire humming, a lone dog howling, Big Papa snoring from the room across the hall.

Sitting up, I see the room and its contents clearly, for the moon gives light through the row of windows facing the bed. I don't belong here. The room is a din-

ing room and not a bedroom. I am in Big Papa and Granny's house in Louisiana, and I am staying here just for a while, I think. But I am not going back to Mother, Daddy said, so maybe I am here for good. I don't know. No one ever talks about Mother.

On the wall across from the bed I see the mahogany china cabinet, where the good dishes are kept. They are never used, they are just to look at. In the bottom drawer Granny stores her own special slips and nightgowns should she ever get sick and have to go decent to the hospital. I look at the sideboard, where the serving dishes and the sterling silver are kept, and then at the big dining table, dark and shining, surrounded by six massive chairs, in the center of the room. This is no place for children.

On the table is my underwear—panties and undershirts and a slip—neatly folded and stacked. Next to it is Donna's underwear, which I have folded and put beside my own. Aunt Mellie promised a small chest of drawers—that would be nice, I could put my things in two drawers and Donna could put hers in two, and the room would seem more like a bedroom.

I lie back down and snuggle my face into the cover. Another memory shuffles in, from way back. I remember Mother singing me to sleep in the rocking chair. I was held, I was safe. She sang a song about soldiers—let's see—"little soldier's had a busy day," that's it, that's the end. Her voice was deep, low for a mommy. Her hands were on my face, my hair, she stroked my hair, I think. Yes, I think she did stroke my hair and my face when she rocked me. I would be almost asleep, and she would carry me to bed and tuck my blue blanket close round me. And I think she kissed me then. Probably she did. Yes, I think she did.

———

Since my father was the only remaining parent, keeping him safe and happy was of paramount concern. I was driven to goodness—or at least to its semblance—to insure that he would not be lost to us: if I could be good enough, Daddy would come back home from his escapades alive. Drunk, maybe, but alive. My careful goodness was offered to remit his public badness and the family's shame.

We lived in a small North Louisiana town that allowed no sale of alcohol. Good people did not drink, and my father was a drunk. He got bootleg liquor at Pee Wee's filling station, catty-corner from the looming white columns of the First Baptist Church. He hung out with unsavory companions, men known to be violent at times, and he occasionally drank white lightning, homemade brew that could kill a man. Sometimes he was picked up for drunk driving and would end up in jail for a few days. Other times he left home for several days running, and we had no idea where he was, didn't know whether he was dead or alive.

My excessive virtue seemed a fair trade that brought some kind of balance and order to the universe, and I gladly took it on, for him. With rough good looks and considerable charm, he was kind of a Johnny Cash without June Carter and Jesus to keep him straight. He had a beautiful man's body that came from his hard work in the oil field. I watched him stretched out on the bed in the back bedroom, stripped to his shorts in the heat, one arm reaching up behind his head, resting from his labor. I adored him.

I was thirteen years old and in the eighth grade when it happened for the first time—the fire in my body, I mean. Henry, the Baptist preacher's son, played last chair second cornet, and I played first chair, third. The stage was crowded, and on that day I found his left thigh pressed tightly against my right thigh as we played "Stars and Stripes Forever." Soon, for no reason that was apparent to me, my right thigh began to feel warm, and then strange waves of heat began to travel from there all through my body. My heart started pounding wildly, and I was thankful that no one could hear it over the music. My face and neck were flushed, and so was Henry's. But of course he was playing his instrument, and his face was always flushed when he played. *Was the same fire burning in him that was burning in me? How could it be other?*

This compelling new experience erased from my mind forevermore my fixation on the pony. I was in love. But if Henry was in love with me, he certainly never indicated it. He never held my hand or asked me to go to the movies with him, nor did he sit beside me on the band bus. He did, however, keep his left thigh firmly pressed against my right thigh during band practice every day at fifth period. That was enough. I continued to be in love with him even after his father got called to a larger church with a bigger salary, and the family left town. I went to the goodbye reception for them but never got close enough to speak to Henry. And what would I have said, anyway? As the family left the reception, I noted that Henry threw his boutonniere, a sweet-smelling gardenia, into the wastebasket. I fished it out and pinned it to the bulletin board in my bedroom, and there it stayed for two years, gathering dust and keeping memory alive.

I tried to pray about these strange new compulsions in my body, about my longing for fleshly love. But every time I started, I felt a stone wall come up between God and me. I didn't know why the wall came, but it rose up so dark and hard that I knew it was real. *Dear God, do you think I could possibly* . . . NO! *Dear God, please help me to* . . . NO! *Dear God, why do you fill me with this need, if I can't* . . . NO! God did not want to discuss the matter at all. It seemed that my visceral self was set fast in opposition to my spiritual being. I wanted love more than anything, maybe even more than God. Why, oh why, did the Holy One make me the lustful, yearning girl that I was?

⁓

I have just gotten back from the mall near my home. The Gap, Victoria's Secret, Hallmark Cards, the usual. It's summer—an unusually hot summer for Oregon—and I have taken to walking in the mall for exercise, and for a respite from the heat. There I notice the teenage girls, with their low-slung jeans and cut-off Ts, tossing their long, shiny hair, whispering and giggling as they meander along, pretending not to notice the boys; and the boys, with their baggy pants and oversized shirts, swaggering down the wide aisles with their cohorts, all chin and bravado. Sometimes I see very young couples, shy and urgent.

Today I stop in Nordstrom's for some eye shadow. I come out with eighty-eight dollars' worth of cosmetics. As I leave the store and ride the escalator to the next level for a frozen yogurt (I trade exercise for food), I think about the cosmetics I did not intend to buy, and I ask myself, "Why are you spending your money this way?" I understand that I am after the same thing these young people are after—the magic. That which takes us out of ourselves. The promise of love serving as a small island amidst the inevitable loneliness and loss in our lives. The connection that makes us forget and hope.

I want to be ready when he comes along. *Who is this "he" I mention? You know*—the one. The man I've been waiting for all my life. The promised one. *I can't believe I'm being so petty—fantasizing about waking up next to someone I love, turning and touching him—when I should by all rights be praying for world peace, or at the very least, campaign finance reform. It's just that a promise is a promise, and this one goes so deeply into my flesh. I so want to be held, to fall sleep in someone's arms.*

This man has been the sticking point for my ongoing feud with God. I have been on my knees, weeping. I have shaken my fist in the air, in a rage. Since thirteen, I have been waiting. Over the produce at the grocery, in the neighborhood bookstore, I see an interesting man—I wonder, *are you the one? Are you?*

But when I am honest with myself, I know that I must take some measure of responsibility. I would have to say that I haven't been ready to love until quite recently. Even if *the man* had shown up at my front door, ringing the bell and greeting me, hat in hand, "Hi. Name's John. God sent me," I would have said, "Sorry, I'm busy," and I would have shut the door in his face.

I've been busy, all right. Studying, writing, ministering. Saving the world. Busy is good; busy keeps me safe. I can love my congregants, but professionalism demands that I keep them at a distance. Perfect for me. Busy keeps me distracted from my loneliness and at the same time gives me a reason not to be available. God is just the fall guy. I know that now. The truth is that all these years I've been afraid to love. I've seen how love can hurt. Firsthand. *You just can't depend on it.* But *not* loving—that can hurt so much more. That's the new truth that has begun to color my living.

I have absolutely no grounds for trusting love, I think. But then again, I do. Growing up, I did have people who cared about me. When we arrived in Louisiana, our grandparents took us in. Yes, though they were in their seventies, they took in their wayward son and his three young children—nine, seven, and three, we were.

We came up in a neighborhood where nobody moved away, ever. I knew all the neighbors and all their dogs. I knew all the sins in their families, and they knew all the sins in mine. The good people at First Baptist Church—to whom I had fled from the Catholics— loved me and guided me along. I sang in the choir. Miss Altalene taught me Bible lessons on Sunday morning and later in the week waited on me when I bought fabric at White's Dry Goods. I was close friends with Janet and Brenda White, the owners' daughters. My teachers saw that I was eager to learn and studious, and they liked me. When I was sick, one of the doctor brothers—Dr. Pat or Dr. James—came to our home and held my hand and asked me how I was and took my temperature. My aunts and uncles were always there on holidays, the aunts preparing food and laughing over some nonsense until tears came, the men in the living room, smoking and telling tales. The fabric was woven. I had that village it takes to raise a child. Bless those people.

Still, my mother's absence was a great presence in my life. I didn't think about her much—in fact, I resented her: she was usually drunk and angry when she called. She sent birthday and Christmas gifts—frilly dresses for the tall, knobby-kneed colt I had become. I wanted her to disappear from my life. I didn't know what exactly I was missing, I just knew I felt different, pushed aside, unworthy.

As I grew into an adult, I learned to invite female friends into my life, but loving a man—that's qualitatively different. My father had five wives in all before he died of alcohol dementia after years of decline in the state hospital. In the final few years of his life, he did not know even his own children. I remember his last clear message to me.

My brother and sister and I are there visiting, and we decide to wheel Daddy outside on the grounds. He is still and gray, and seems more dead than alive. Some kind of construction is underway; red clay earth shows up like a great bloody gash in the green grass. My brother keeps making videos of the pathetic scene, and I begin to have the eerie sensation that I am in a very bad movie. Newly ordained, I am trying in vain to tell my father that I have become a minister. "I'm a minister, Daddy." He squints his eyes at the sun, trying to understand. I raise my voice and say again, "I'm a minister, Daddy." Still nothing. I raise my voice even louder, I practically yell at him, "Daddy, I'm a preacher!"

"Give 'em hell," he says, and for just a second that old glint comes into his eyes once again. My bad boy.

Though love has been so deeply suspect for me, since that day in band my flesh has continued to be subversive to my fears, and I keep being drawn to men. Through the years, there have been men for whom I have cared deeply. I have been sexually bonded with men. I was engaged to three (sequentially, all doctors); I married and later divorced the third, who was and is quite a good man. But I had never been *in love,* meaning I had never really made myself emotionally vulnerable to a man. I had always held back, had always been with men who wanted me more than I wanted them, or younger men who were passionate but not quite grown up in one way or another, men who could never have much power over me, men I knew I would leave at some point. *I will never need anyone so much again.*

And then there was another barrier to my loving. Having not been attended to properly during my younger days, I grew up convinced that there was something dreadfully wrong with me—else why would I have been so disregarded? With the narcissism of the child, I had internalized the notion that I did not deserve to be loved, and what was worse, that I myself could not love. *Well, then, let me be respected. I will work twice as hard, give twice as much as the next person. And I will be good. I will be perfect, "even as my Father in heaven is perfect." I will earn my right to be on this earth.*

I fling all this evidence—my relentless work, my (largely imagined) goodness—at my angel. When I want to play dirty, I fling my suffering as well. *How could you?* I bargain with my angel. *I've done my part. Now I want my due. Collection time.* All of a sudden I'm in a headlock, and I find myself thrown to the floor, my nose pushed out of shape, my arm twisted behind my back. "We don't deal here," my angel whispers in my ear. "Get it?"

"OK, OK, I get it," I answer, but when he eases up on his hold, I elbow him in the solar plexus, bite his hand, and flip him over, tossing his halo askew, sending feathers flying. "Listen, you—I won't let you go till you bless me."

He grunts and struggles, but I hold on. Finally his wings tire and he sighs, "All right, let's talk this over."

I grit my teeth. "I want the blessing," I say, as I release him.

He sits on the ground opposite me, legs spread, wings akimbo, resting, a distinct frown on his otherwise angelic face. "You don't understand, you silly human," he says. "You have been blessed from the time of your conception. Your mother and your father, oh, how they did love! Their love was consecrated. Every breath you take is a gift. Your very longing for love is a gift. Your passion. Your caring. All gifts. Now listen up: What God wants from you is, first, thanksgiving, and then, just companionship. God gets so lonely at times. I bet you didn't know that. When was the last time you were in touch?

"Oh," I say and pull up a memory.

—

I find myself feeling quite desperate at one point during my theological studies. Guilty. Separated from God. I decide to make a cold call to Father Dan O'Hanlon, a priest someone had told me was "deeply spiritual" and who sometimes served students as a spiritual director. He answers and, hesitating, I dare to ask him if he will talk with me. He says yes, but he can meet with me only once, because he is ill and does not have much energy. So I go. I knock, and he opens the door and welcomes me. His room is furnished with only a small table, two chairs, and a single bed, all of the plainest and simplest sort. Kind of Shaker/Catholic. Father O'Hanlon has dark eyes that seem to penetrate the sham that my goodness has become, and yet the eyes are kind. I sit in one of the chairs, a rocker, and rock and rock and pour out my story. My prayers are going nowhere, I tell him. Just to the ceiling, and no further. I go on and on, pausing just to wipe the tears that begin flooding my face and refuse to stop. Finally all my words have spilled out. He allows for a time of silence. Then he speaks. He says, "Prayer is not about changing God; prayer is about being with God." Several months later I hear he is dead. Some virus he caught in Africa.

—

My angel waited for me to drift back from my musings, and then he said, gently, as he touched my knee, "Look, it's bigger than you know. Bigger than you *can* know. Trust me. Everything is as it should be. It can't be other than it is, at this moment. Don't fret."

Is that it? Is that all? I blink, and my angel is gone. . . .

Four months later I allow myself to fall in love for the first time. It was a surrender I had never before experienced. I had known this man casually for about two years, but had never thought of him as someone with whom I might become intimate. Didn't occur to me. But then we found ourselves having a beer in a neighborhood restaurant one evening, and it did occur to me, and I saw that he was beautiful, and I was a goner. A few weeks after that, we fell breathlessly into bed, and I was totally swept away.

Sex for me became the ecstasy I always knew it could be. When we made love, I became every woman who had ever loved, and to me, he became every man, and our union was the union of all lovers, throughout time. Age had no meaning, beauty was no measure. I was freed, during our lovemaking at least, from the prison of self.

We were always eager, always joyous, when we reached for each other. It was often similar, the ways we pleasured each other, but it was always new, for me at least, because I was there and no place else, and I brought all of myself to our bed. All of me came alive. Every touch, every kiss held both its very own sweetness and the promise of what was coming next. I knew that my taking him in was a great comfort to him, and I held him there, and my giving felt pure, felt sacred. Some broken-off part of me felt restored. Then we would talk, sometimes for a few minutes, sometimes long into the night. For him, that was the most intimate part, he said. That's the part he had never done before, he said.

For me, I could not imagine anything more intimate or more satisfying than having his body inside my body. Than loving him. "It's quite a miracle," I said one night as we were lying there together.

"What is?" he asked.

"It's quite a miracle, what happens between a man and a woman."

Turns out, though, that this man I loved did not love me. He wanted to. He tried to. I'm the sort of woman he told himself he *should* love—but he just didn't and couldn't. "I don't love you enough," he would say. And finally, after eighteen months, I had to agree, *he doesn't love me enough,* and I left him. How could we part, you might ask. I sometimes still ask myself the same question. I missed him terribly for a very long time. Sometimes, even after two years, the wanting sneaks up on me again, unbidden, throwing me off balance.

I no longer fret and complain to God, though, about lacking a partner. It's not that I wouldn't like the closeness, the companionship. It's not that I don't long for the lovemaking. I do. But in a larger sense, it doesn't—it can't—matter. No demands, no petulant prayers thrown up to heaven. Love is a gift of grace, not an entitlement, and we can't order it up the way we can a good Chinese takeout. We may have to remain hungry. Or not. I know this: as soon as demand moves in, love moves out. I'm learning to live, as St. Paul advised, in whatever state I find myself. No assurances. Only raw faith.

Who would I be, if not a passionate, angry woman? I'm moving into the answer now: I would be a given over woman. The passion without so much of the ego. The anger shifting strangely to compassion, as I understand how much longing fills all human hearts, and how much suffering we all endure. And stranger yet, I sense that all these feelings are converging in a nameless kind of joy. How can I tell you of it? It's the joy of acceptance, of relief, a letting go of the tension between what I have demanded of life and what I find is true of life. Bringing together what I want and what I have been offered. Being at one with what is.

What I see now is that love is all around me, opportunities abide —and love is ultimately all of a piece. There are many ways to touch and be touched. I'm not talking here about a poor substitute for the real thing—I'm talking about different manifestations of the real thing.

When I pray now, I grow weary of words. And yet contemplative prayer is difficult for me. Just being with the Holy One can't be enough, can it? Trying to meditate, I'm restless. I still want to be *doing*, still believe I need to earn my right to feel the comfort of the sun on my skin. I fall into depression at times, and when I'm there, the world seems empty. I know, though, beyond any doubt, that I can love. Lucky me. Some great chasm of the heart has been healed.

Thankfulness rises up in me spontaneously when I look at the colors on my dinner plate before I eat: the greenness of the green beans, the amazing yellow of the squash; or when I touch a rose to the forehead of one of our babies during a child dedication service at the church; or when my friend's new pug puppy jumps into my arms and I feel its warmth on my body and it licks my face all over. Ordinary blessings.

Four words now form the core of my spoken prayer life: "I'm available. What's next?" I do not say these words in resignation, like some galley slave or indentured servant. They arise from curiosity and, ironically, a playful spirit. "What's next?" My trickster God, my lovely Coyote, is full of surprises.

Fearless

SUSAN GRIFFIN

❧

Within our darkness there is not one place for
Beauty. The whole place is for Beauty.
RENÉ CHAR, *Leaves of Hypnos,*
a War Journal (1943–44)[1]

In the first days of the war, it is hard to defend oneself against ugliness. On the TV screen, the pronouncements of military leaders and embedded journalists have a flat quality, whether from indifference to suffering, or indifference to truth, one cannot say. The rain of dispatches filled with contradictions, lies, and hypocrisies urge violence, and while we are presented with chillingly banal accounts of massive bombardment—advertised as the "shock and awe" campaign—an ugly state of mind prevails. Even the anger I feel in response feels ugly. It is a corrosive anger, which aligns itself with fear: the fear that nuclear weapons, biological weapons, or chemical weapons will be used by either side; that this violence will ignite a third World War or a fierce new wave of terrorist attacks; that the economy, already weak, will collapse; and underneath all this, a pervasive fear of loss and death.

What can fearlessness mean in such a time? The notion of feeling no fear usually distresses me. I think of this state of mind as ignorant or foolhardy, the product of an adolescent failure to comprehend mortality or a dissociated state of mind. In his work on the psychology of combat, Glen Gray writes that experienced soldiers have learned to distrust those men who know no fear. Such men are not only suicidal but dangerous to their compatriots. Glenn describes such unwavering fearlessness as a symptom of psychosis.

I do not think of myself as particularly brave. Ordinarily I go in the other direction, worrying over more safety and health issues than can be listed, including whether I will get enough sleep on any given night, if I will have enough to eat or money to pay my bills. I am not drawn to challenging sports such as downhill skiing. I like to swim in calm waters and sleep in a comfortable bed.

Yet this year I found a new capaciousness within myself, bearing a different kind of fearlessness. It was just before the start of the war in March, on International Women's Day, after speaking at a rally against the war on Iraq and then marching through the capital, that I found myself, for a few blessed hours, relatively free of the small fears that plague me.

I was grateful to speak at the rally. Though some consider speaking out to be courageous, this comes naturally to me. It is something I have done for years without much reservation. In a sense, it is harder for me to keep quiet than to speak to a large crowd. Yet the protest was not a casual event for me. The thought that such deaths were about to occur on a massive scale had been troubling my sleep. The words I said at the rally that day came through the same nighttime door by which many poems arrive, traveling like siren songs from some mysterious part of consciousness, beyond ordinary knowledge. But if at times such messages are seductive, this time they were filled with an undeniable anguish, as if they were cries for help and warnings all at once.

For months whenever I thought about the course my country was taking and the suffering on both sides this war would cause, I would be seized with an almost savage grief. Yet throughout this particular day in early March, when tears welled up in my eyes, they were not just tears of sorrow. They came instead from a complex mix of emotions in which joy and sorrow do not contradict, an elusive state of mind. The word that comes to mind now is *beauty*.

And if I am thinking of beautiful *music* now, it is partly because the night before the rally when together with my friend Alice Walker I was driven into Washington D.C., we chanced to hear the voice of Mahalia Jackson on the radio. It was this voice, powerful beyond what can easily be named, that paced our journey past the Lincoln memorial, the Capitol building, and the Washington monument into the city. This journey was to be an augury of what we would experience all the next day, as we spoke and marched and then crossed the police barricades around the White House, having decided minutes before that we were willing to break the law if needed. To make our protest of the coming war visible, we were willing to commit civil disobedience.

As we approached the White House, Mahalia Jackson's voice was still fresh in my memory. She sings gospel, which she learned to do in church, and you can hear it in the sound of her voice. Human beings are creatures of interdependence; circumstances, where we live, structures, especially sanctuaries of all kinds, including churches, shape us and affect how we live. Such buildings are constructed to serve and amplify the voices of those who congregate in them. When you sing in such a place, you can hear echoes from the walls, and this will often cause your voice to take on a deeper, sometimes sad or even fervent tonality. In turn, amplified by the resonant sounds of choirs, the voices of the assembled crowd, your spirit too will grow larger.

We sang together as we stood on the newly illegal ground in front of the White House. Rachel Bagby taught us some quick and easy harmonies. Aside from Rachel's radiantly beautiful voice, we did nothing that was all that new or creative musically. Some of us sang off-key. Many of the songs were ones we had known for a long time, learned at other protests. But the music was thrilling nonetheless because in truth we had entered a sanctuary, albeit one created on the spot, a temporary, mobile structure but remarkably effective. And if our gathering made our protest against the war more audible, it also made my spirit grow large.

This was not the first time I have taken part in a protest. I began when I was seventeen years old, joining a march that called for banning the atomic weapons. Over the following forty-three years I have been part of demonstrations for civil rights, against the Vietnam War, for freedom of speech, against McCarthyism, for countless feminist causes, for the right to abortion, and for gay rights. In all these protests I felt the presence of what for want of a better name we call *spirit*. Many modern political movements have had a strongly spiritual dimension. Countless leaders for social justice have included prayer and meditation in their work. One thinks of Gandhi, Martin Luther King, Rosa Parks, Dorothy Day, Cesar Chavez, Dolores Huerta, Simone Weil, Dietrich Bonhoeffer, the Berrigan brothers, Joanna Macy, Starhawk. The spiritual presence I have felt while protesting has often been stronger than my experience of such a presence in any of the places of worship I have sought out over the years, whether churches, synagogues, or Buddhist temples. Why this is I cannot easily say. But as we sang "We Shall Overcome" on that March day, I could feel a bodily knowledge of the courage that inspired that song and the oppression that made that courage necessary.

I am well aware as I write that the combination of spirituality and politics is not without problems. When I was a young woman, most of us who were part of the student movement were suspicious of religion. Not only did we inherit the anticlerical sentiments of the French and American Revolutions, and the idea that religion merely distracts people from injustice, we had in our minds the all too recent images of massive crowds whipped into a hysterical frenzy in their irrational worship of Hitler. And now the rise of religious fundamentalism, on both the American right and around the world, presents another more frightening picture of the mixture of religion and politics.

Yet over time I have witnessed in myself and others of my generation a reclamation of spiritual experience. Through the transformations of older religions, the revival of lost traditions and the invention of new practices, or through a direct relationship with the larger dimensions of existence, gradually a sense of common cause with all living beings, of sharing one planet comprising one ecological body, has arisen among many of those among my generation who are most committed to social justice. Having touched on what is as much an experience as an insight, I can see a clear difference between the religious approaches that lead to violence and those that lead to communion. The first, defined by rage and hatred, creates delusional ideas of reality that cause definitive, seemingly unbridgeable divisions among us. The second encourages inner peace, compassion, truth telling, and reconciliation.

During the months before the war on Iraq I attended many powerful and moving rallies. But a couple of these were disappointing, even alienating, not only to me, but to many of those who assembled to demand peace. I remember feeling assaulted by rage-filled voices and long haranguing speeches that failed to touch me. Anger, even rage, in response to an unnecessary war is legitimate. But if we are to create a real alternative to violence, some alchemical process must take place among us. In the deepest recesses of inner experience, the great power and beauty of peace must be made manifest.

In this way, the day last March I spent in Washington, which began with a rally, and ended in civil disobedience, entered my spirit so deeply that in the end I felt as if I had undergone some mysterious sea change that even now continues to unfold inside me.

For a temporary sanctuary to be built out of an assembly of a few friends and many strangers, a certain magic must be present, an earthly miracle that is ultimately unpredictable. And yet in conjuring such a phenomenon, there is great skill involved, even recipes. Accomplished organizers created the ground for this miracle from many ingredients. There was the wit and humor of the name the organization adopted from the beginning, *Code Pink,* a parody of the color code used for "homeland security." Over time the clothes, shawls, scarves, hats of hot pink that women and men who were part of the vigil wore became wilder and funnier, creating a significant crack in the heavy sense of powerlessness and doom so many felt. Yet none of this humor belied the gravity of what was about to occur. A contingent of women from Code Pink went to Iraq to talk with ordinary Iraqi citizens and meet with Iraqi women's groups. They brought the real dimensions of shock and awe, of missiles and bombs, home. Modeling what the Vietnamese Buddhist teacher Thich Nat Hahn would say, "being peace," they spent months conducting a vigil outside the White House, standing all day, often in rain or snow and bitter cold.

An extraordinary meeting preceded the formation of this organization. In May of the previous year, thirty-six women from across the country came together for a long weekend to discuss the state of the world. Activists, writers, spiritual leaders who had worked with a range of issues, from the quality of food available to residents of

Watts and East Oakland, to the rights of immigrants, to pollution of air, water, and earth, to the threat of war. Over five days, as we shuddered and wept over the state of our world, we wove a connection between one another and all the issues we discussed. The idea for "code pink" came from this weave, a fabric made of communion.

All this was in the sanctuary we shared and it gave us a rare kind of safety. Not safety from violence precisely but from the subtle, daily violence to our hearts and minds that has allowed so many to accept what is unacceptable. Thus, together on that day, one could feel the full dimensionality of the terrible song, which had in myriad ways been keeping so many awake at night. We were all hearing it.

The realization was thick and palpable and made me weak in the knees with its force. Paradoxically I felt more than a modicum of relief that the dimensions of violence and terror were revealed here, understood not just as facts, but as emotional, flesh-and-blood consequence. So as nearly twenty thousand women marched the nearly three miles to Lafayette Park, creating a hot-pink ribbon through the city that made countless passing cars honk and pedestrians smile and wave and flash the peace sign at us, my harrying worry, muffled fear, the ragged shrieks of nightmare and horror dogging my mood began to mix and mutate into something beautiful. The tears that kept coming into my eyes had a measure of joy in them. To see this side of humanity, able to imagine and consider the affliction and suffering of others.

The decision to go past the barricades was quick. I have never been eager to see the inside of a jail cell. I was arrested once as part of a writers' demonstration for protesting apartheid. Alice was there on that day too. While Maya Angelou sang to us, we all sat on the floor in a corridor at the University of California, trying to block the door and waiting to be processed. One by one we were led through an assembly line, fingerprinted, photographed, asked to sign some papers, and then sent home. This time, I knew, it would not be quite so easy.

But in the same way that late at night I have on a few occasions found myself ignoring every symptom of fatigue to stay up talking, dancing, or making love, I could not stop myself from this course of action. It felt good. Despite having had little sleep and virtually no food all day, my body was leaning in the direction of those barricades. I was truly gladdened to pass over them.

The fearlessness, which had been growing in me all day, took a quantum leap then. I felt light. "Giddy" someone who heard me on the radio said. We were being interviewed as we stood in that forbidden space, in front of our president's house, holding hands, swaying to the sound of our voices. After talking with other women who were arrested that day, it seems that most if not all of us were flooded with a mysterious joy.

I have heard the concept explained in various texts handed down by visionaries and mystics in many different spiritual traditions. When I lost someone very close to me, in the weeks after her death I gained a momentary understanding that happiness and sorrow are not different, that life is seamless and filled with an extraordinary love that seems to pour right out of the air itself. It is what the Buddhists call enlightenment, and though I am not an enlightened being, I can tell you that this *is* real; I experienced it again on that day I was arrested for going too close to the White House fence.

Is that why despite my hunger and fatigue and the fact that I could no longer bend my sixty-year-old arthritic knees, all during our arrest and the three hours it took to get us paddy wagons, according to the friends who witnessed me, I had such a fearless expression on my face? I was not entirely free of anxiety. I wondered how long they would hold us. I thought for an instant or two about my airplane ticket and the appointments I had back home. But the sun was out and we were all in good humor, glad to be together. Maxine Hong Kingston's face was radiant. Alice was smiling in a famously whimsical way. Nina Utne's eyes were glistening. When Terry Tempest Williams started to leave, she lingered, had trouble tearing herself away, and then stayed.

And then the day had its own comic aspects. Once we stood in front of the White House we were told we had to move, and then after we had stood our ground for a while, we witnessed a sudden flurry of police activity. Brigades appeared; uniformed men stood in columns, feet apart, shoulders back. The officer returned to give us a five-minute warning. Still we did not move except to sway back and forth, swaying as we sang "Give Peace a Chance," helped along in our harmonies by Rachel's glorious voice.

Strangely peaceful, despite frequent displays of raw power staged in front of us, we smiled as we waited to be arrested. Years of spiritual practice had helped me understand, at least in theory, that making enemies only leads to greater suffering. In contrast to the way so many called the police "pigs" at protests held in the sixties, this understanding was intrinsic to the way the march was organized. Even while disobeying their orders, we treated the police women and men with respect. In turn, two of them asked us for peace buttons.

Because some of the men who appeared in helmets and riot gear seemed particularly menacing I was tempted at times to express defiance. But instead I tried to imagine what they must have been like as infants, a task which, since I have two small grandchildren, was not difficult. So by whatever means necessary we continued to smile and sing as we waited. And waited, and waited. Five minutes, ten, twenty, forty minutes passed. Until finally we realized there were no more columns, in fact there were hardly any police there at all any longer. We were still there but they had dispersed.

But by now, because we were not only willing but resolved to be arrested, very slowly we began to move backwards past the yellow tape that cordoned off Pennsylvania Avenue from the sidewalk in front of the White House. Once on the sidewalk, the whole program repeated, warnings and columns, this time with police in different, slightly more menacing regalia, warning again, followed by another five-minute deadline that stretched out to over forty minutes, and finally, the police had once again dispersed.

It was only after we moved still farther back, to the zone right in front of the fence that has been illegal since 9/11, that finally, without fanfare and with the greatest politeness and consideration, the arrests finally began. In the annals of resistance, we were not especially heroic. We were not mistreated. There was of course discomfort. It was 6 p.m. We had spoken and given interviews and marched two miles and we were all tired. The sun was going down. Alice had left her coat with someone and was cold. Beginning to suffer the symptoms of a chronic illness I have had for years, my hands and face were turning numb. Nevertheless we were happy and, it is true, we were fearless.

Fearless. It is a state of mind, I have concluded, that in its natural state is more aligned to peace than war. What made me courageous that day was that for a few hours I was living in a state of peace. It is a mood, a cast of mind, that can be created in any assembly, an atmosphere as real as the one created over our planet by the exhaling of trees and plants, and it is, in the end, the only source of hope. Peace the ground of fearlessness, in peace the seeds of courage.

Is it unrealistic or grandiose to believe that the ugliness that dogs our days is not inevitable? Or does the grandiosity lie elsewhere, in plans designed to force others toward a world order we claim will be peaceful? Is it far-fetched to think beauty belongs to us still just as it did in the eleventh century, when the Japanese poet Izumi Shikibu wrote,

Watching the moon,
at midnight
solitary, mid-sky
I knew myself completely,
no part left out.[2]

The war starts. My friend the activist Jodie Evans writes to me, *My heart is broken and there is so much to do.* The violence continues. Children, soldiers just barely grown, start to die, while so much beauty waits within us.

1. René Char wrote this long prose poem during the years he was part of the *Maquis*, the French resistance against the Nazi occupation of France.

2. "Watching the Moon," by Izumi Shikibu, translation by Jane Hirshfield and Mariko Aratani. From *Women in Praise of the Sacred*, ed. Jane Hirshfield (New York: HarperCollins, 1994).

Death of a Mouse

M.F.K. FISHER

Before I try to start work again after several weeks of illness and convalescence, I think I should make some sort of report on the surprising attempt of my soul to reappear. Perhaps I should call this report
"Notes Found in an Empty Achromycin Bottle," although the actual
encounter with my soul for the second time, as well as my sudden
ability to recall the first one, happened before I began taking the
pills.

I knew for some time that I did not feel well, but I had no idea
that I would become so defined by pain and fever that I could be
near such an experience as the one I had. Four days and nights of the
white tablets emptied the little bottle, and I was pronounced ready to
begin to recover.

The recovery has been interesting and lengthy, and while it still
goes on I feel impatient of the waste of time and of myself, and yet almost voluptuously, I cling to the need for sleep and miss the cosmic
mouse that squeaked to me in my left lung when I was alone and
wandering.

Now I am nearly well again, and must begin to stay upright and
make the correct moves in the right directions, and not wonder too
much about when my soul will come again.

Physical illness is ugly and I shall speak of it as little as possible,
and only in connection with the other thing.

Apparently I was really ill, and like most stubborn healthy people I was incredulous about it, so that I waited several days before I admitted that I could not get up and make breakfast for my family, and then spent five days in bed before I started to cry when I confessed that I needed a doctor's help, no matter how pill laden and generally unwelcome.

The night before I made this last feverish pain-stiff admission, I coughed steadily in a small dry exhausting way, perhaps a little more so than for the previous long time. It seemed by then a normal way of existing. The poor body was at once all-absorbing in the energy it demanded but at the same time almost despicably unimportant, thanks to long fasting. I listened to the cough, always on the same level of sound and effort, with a detached recognition. Brother Cough, I said philosophically, as to a longtime companion. Friend Squeak, I said affectionately, for it was the mouse living in my dark hot lung-cabin with the rigid roof beams and the walls so tinder dry that comforted me with thin songs and chatter.

Then that night the speed and sound of the cough changed, and the mouse multiplied into mad rats eating me. And up into my throat moved my soul.

I got out of bed, as if to meet it courteously.

Dreadful sounds were coming from me.

The soul, smooth and about the size of a small truffle or scallop or a large marble, rose firmly into my upper throat. It cut off my wind, but that did not matter for the time we both needed.

I knew what it looked like, for I had seen it long ago. I knew its color and its contours and its taste, for I had held it in my hand once and studied it and then chewed and swallowed it to wait within me. But this was not the time for its return.

"Go back," I cried out to it, in language it recognized through the wild coughing, and through the way the bloody rats scrabbled behind it to escape with all of me dragging from their teeth, with my lungs my liver my guts all waiting torn and ready to stream out like flags behind them, if my soul should flee first, leaving only bones and shell and the little mouse.

"Go back," I begged ferociously as it stayed there for years that night, turning slightly as breath pushed it and the rats waited. It was interesting to feel it turn, for I remembered its shape, pure and smooth in my red gullet.

There was very little left now, of the breath it had trapped behind it with the rats, and indeed of me the fighter. It seemed as if most of my solar plexus had been torn loose by the impatient invaders. If the soul left me then, I feared fastidiously that I would seem to be vomiting, but it would be *me*, not some extraneous thing like fried fish wolfed in a greasy restaurant. It would be unworthy.

"*NO*. No, *wait*," I begged it, and I promised to accept the next visit it would pay me, and I reminded it of our long years together.

I told it, in a flash as long as the eon of time it takes for one molecule to wed another, of our first meeting, and of the mystery and respect and indeed affection I had battened on from that day.

I was about five, maybe four. It was a beautiful morning, maybe spring or winter but good, maybe a Saturday. I lay in my bed waiting for my little sister to awaken, studying the white painted iron of the bedsteads. Surely there were birds talking, and curtains stirring in the windows of the pleasant room, and sounds from downstairs, but all I remember is that in a ruthless slow way, but without any pain or fear for me, my young small soul rose up into my throat and then came out.

I did not choke. I did not spit it out. It simply rose from inside me, glided along the root and the rest of my tongue, and then lay in the palm of my hand, which must have been waiting for it in front of my mouth. I was dazzled and yet unastounded.

It was about as big as a little hazelnut or chickpea, of the subtlest creamy white, like ivory but deeper. It was delicately convoluted, like the carvings on a human brain or a monkey's, but worn by thousands of years to its present silkiness without ever being in danger of turning into a ball or egg. It was perfection in form.

Nothing has ever been seen so clearly by my mind's eye, I think. I still know the simplicity and the yellowish shadows in the whorls of its surface, and my hand behind it with the skin infinitely crude and coarse and lined, the fresh palm of a child.

I held the thing carefully for what were probably only a few seconds. I recognized it fully, without any doubt or timidity, as my own soul. Then I put it gently into my mouth, bit into it, and chewed and swallowed it.

It had nothing to do with food or even nourishment, being without taste, and moist, but at the same time almost floury.

I made sure that none had stayed in my mouth and that all of it was well down my throat, for it was important that it reassemble itself and stay there inside me, to grow. I knew that I would see it again, just as I knew that something very important had happened to me, perhaps the first since being born. It was in a way like becoming a person instead of a creature, woman instead of baby, big instead of little. I was myself, *me*, and I had seen and touched the proof of it. I had been shown.

The good day unfolded like all other days before me, the happy child, but of course I was different, for I had a core now.

For many years, I occasionally remembered this, but without any questioning at all. I never wondered about its next visit, but I knew there would be one, just as I knew that people would tell me it was a little accident of bodily secretion or digestion, or a dream, if I talked of it.

But the night that it did come again was a mistake, except for the reassurance that it was still there.

It was as if I thought this occasion unworthy of it. I was befouled by fever; the different parts of me seemed to be sending off almost visible fumes and stinking gases, when I would choose to be silk and sweet oils for it. The rats were behind it, trailing their shreds of my tissue, my lining, my guts, and still ripping and gnawing at me with their filthy teeth as I coughed passionately in the middle of the black room by my bed. It was ugly, my state.

"Go back," I screamed, as my soul rose like a smooth nut in my throat.

It had grown since our first meeting. Some of the convolutions of its polished carving had worn even fainter since I'd seen it like a little quiet keepsake in my hand, pearly but not gleaming, wet but not slippery, ivory colored but not dull.

It sickened me that I must ask it to return to the bloody mob below, yet I knew with all my tattered force that it was not yet time to hold it in my hand again, and that I could not do so with dignity.

There was no clash of wills between us, certainly, but I learned something of eternity before it did withdraw.

I hate to think of it then in the red caves and the long flaming tunnels, for that was a bad night for it and me.

The next day I asked for help, being in a state of exhaustion that I could never try to explain to anyone. A professionally kind stranger came and left some advice and some fresh courage, and the Achromycin pills in a little bottle, to drive out the mouse in my left lung.

I felt sorry about that. But it was the mouse or me, the doctor said, and I am important because the next time my soul shows up, I must be in good shape to welcome it. I may be very old, with no teeth to chew it, no juice left to swallow it, but I shall catch it in the palm of my hand as I did when I was a child, and this time let it lead me.

Santa Teresa

*Notes on a spiritual genius and her powerful prayer
and character, which refresh us to this day.*

TERRY TEMPEST WILLIAMS

On the train to Avila, tamarisks are in bloom. Pines. Junipers. Arid
shrub country pocketed with boulders. Magpies. Poppies. The *meseta*
or plateau country of central Spain looks much like my home in the
American Southwest.

The medieval walls surrounding the *ciudad antigua,* the old city, of
Avila are the threshold to the world of Santa Teresa in the early six-
teenth century. Even though the walls were built miraculously five
hundred years earlier by 1,900 men in nine years after the town had
been reclaimed from the Moors, it is Teresa's presence that lingers.

Santa Teresa sits outside her city, reposed in white marble, her
gaze directed over her right shoulder, a plume pen in her right hand,
her left hand open to the Mysteries. Hundreds of swifts circle her.
Pink, white, and yellow roses flourish against the stone wall. Someone has left a bouquet of wildflowers at her feet. Overhead three
storks fly toward the bell tower del Carmen where they nest. Did
Santa Teresa know these birds, these mediators between heaven
and earth? These swifts and storks must have swayed her thinking.
Surely the Holy Spirit appears in more incarnations than doves.

To whom do I pray?

A Spanish woman sits in the row across from me in the Iglesia de Santa Teresa reciting her prayers in whispers as she rotates each bead of her rosary through her fingers. Her hands are folded beneath her chin. She alternates her prayers with the reading of scriptures.

To whom do I pray?

I kneel before the statue of Santa Teresa, gilded and animated by the soft light in this small, dark alcove. Her right hand is outstretched as though she were about to touch Spirit, her left hand covers her heart.

I close my eyes and listen.

After many minutes of silence, what comes into my mind is the phrase, "wet not dry."

I close my eyes tighter and concentrate more deeply, let these words simply pass through as one does with distractions in meditation. Again, the words, "wet not dry."

The woman across the aisle from me is weeping. Her private utterings, *"para ti,"* for you, are audible. I open my eyes feeling little emotion and look down at the worn tiles beneath my feet. The Spanish woman faces the Saint, bows, crosses herself and leaves.

Wondering if I should be here at all, I try once again to pray. In the stillness, the phrase returns.

All I can hear in the sanctity of this chapel is what sounds at best like a cheap antiperspirant jingle. Filled with shame, I look up at Santa Teresa's face. Later that afternoon, I steady myself by sitting beneath an old cottonwood tree, similar to the ones I have sat under a hundred times in the desert. I open Santa Teresa's autobiography, *The Life of Saint Teresa of Avila by Herself,* and randomly turn to a page: "...and God converted the dryness of my soul into a great tenderness." I turn another page: "Only once in my life do I remember

asking Him for consolation and that was when I was very dry...."
And another: "It is my opinion that though a soul may seem to be
deriving some immediate benefit when it does anything to further
itself in this prayer of union, it will in fact very quickly fall again,
like a building without foundations.... Remain calm in times of
dryness."

Unknown to me, Santa Teresa's book articulates "the Four Waters of Prayer." She says simply that wetness brings us "to a recol-
lected state." A well. A spring. A fountain. To drink deeply from the
Spirit and quench the aridity of the soul to retrieve, revive and renew
our relationship with God. Where are my tears? Where is the rain? I
ask myself. "I am now speaking of that rain that comes down abun-
dantly from heaven to soak and saturate the whole garden."

The leaves of the cottonwood tree shield me from the heat as I
read her *Confessions* slowly: "Who is this whom all my faculties thus
obey? Who is it that in a moment sheds light amidst such great darkness, who softens a heart that seemed to be of stone and sheds the
water of gentle tears where for so long it had seemed to be dry? Who
gives these desires? Who gives this courage? What have I been thinking of? What am I afraid of?"

The smell of lavender and rosemary collide in the garden. Something breaks open in me. What might it mean to honor thirst before
hunger and joy before obligation? *Una botella de agua. Necesito una botella
de agua.* These are the first words out of my mouth as I awaken from a
dream.

The Monasterio de Encarnación, a dignified granite fortress
north of the Wall, is not far from the *parador* where I am staying. In
1534, Santa Teresa walked through these doors when she was twenty
years old. It is closed. I sit on the stone steps outside the corridor.
Hace calor. I settle in the shade and read more of Santa Teresa's
words: "All its joys came in little sips."

As I continue to read her autobiography, the mystic writes about women and the importance of discretion in speaking of one's spiritual experiences, the need to share with others of like mind for solace and safety, reflection and inspiration.

Joseph Smith believed so fully in Santa Teresa's visions that he had himself sealed in the Carmelite nun in "the everlasting covenant of marriage." He recognized her as a spiritual soulmate, trusting that revelations from God have been and will be continuous through time, that the truth is soul-wrenching, having said himself that he shared only a hundredth of what he saw when the heavens opened up to him. Schooled in the hermetic traditions of Santa Teresa's time, he might have felt as though they were contemporaries, sympathetic to her roving states of mind.

She speaks of her progress in prayer: "It seemed to me that there must either be something very good or something extremely bad about it. I was quite certain that my experiences were supernatural. . . ." Santa Teresa sought the help of a learned cleric. Many had said she was possessed by the devil. He did not. He encouraged her to find her own path of revelation, "to trust oneself in God, in Truth."

I close the book feeling weak, light-headed perhaps because of the heat, perhaps because of the intensity of Santa Teresa's story: a child who at the age of ten vowed to be a nun but at age fourteen blossomed into a vibrant young woman enraptured by the sensory pleasures of the world, gifted in poetry and literature.

She fell tumultuously in love and was so frightened by her own sexuality that she confessed to her father, who immediately sent her to the convent. There, struggling with the disciplined life set by the nuns against her own instinctive nature, she succumbed to violent seizures and bouts of hysteria that eventually left her paralyzed for years, seized by the darkest of visions, unable to move, her pain

barely tolerable. She denounced all medical treatments and relied
solely on prayer, never giving up hope of being healed. At one point,
deep in a coma mistaken for death, the nuns dug a grave for her.
And then the miraculous day arrived. In 1540, she awoke to find
her arms and legs no longer paralyzed. She had successfully passed
through her journey through Hell. Teresa de Avila stood up and
walked. It was proclaimed a miracle, a cure that reached the masses
whereby people from surrounding villages came to see the nun
whom God had healed.

Her life from that point forward was a testament of austere devotion and simplicity, but she never gave up her pen. Inside the Monasterio, there are relics: a wooden log which Santa Teresa used as a
pillow; a small statue of Christ "covered with wounds," which is said
to have been very important to her spiritual awakening of compassion and sorrow; a statue of Saint Joseph, who taught her how to
pray. The nuns have passed down the story that this statue used to
talk to Santa Teresa. When she left on her travels she would leave
him on the prioress's chair. Upon her return, he would tell her everything that had gone on in her absence.

The key to her cell where she lived for twenty-seven years begs to
be turned. Turn the key. Santa Teresa's hands open the door.

Downstairs, there is a tiny revolving door made of oak. It was the
only access the nuns had with the outside world, sending messages
out with one turn and receiving them with another in silence.

I descend further into the stark parlor where San Juan de la Cruz
and Santa Teresa were *"suspendido en éxtasis,"* lifted in ecstasy. Once
again, I sit quietly. The word *"casado"* comes into my mind: marriage, a prayer of union, a state of oneness with God and with whom
we confide our bodies. The Divine Lover. In these moments of pure
union, body, soul, and spirit fuse. Ecstasy. Elevation. Suspension.

The bells of the Monasterio de la Encarnación begin ringing. In the courtyard, two young girls are singing, one is playing the guitar, the other is clapping with her eyes closed. I walk down the road to the plaza where there is a fountain bubbling up from a stone basin and sit down.

Teenagers play in the pool below the fountain. They flirt and splash each other, then the young men and women, soaked, hoist each other up and over the stone wall and disappear. A man interrupts their frolicking to fill two jugs tied together by a rope that he swings over his neck.

The small plaza is quiet. I walk to the fountain and wash my face and hands and arms. The water is cold and invigorating. I wash my face again.

An old man with a black beret dressed in a white shirt with an olive green cardigan and grey slacks comes to the fountain carrying a plastic sack with two gallon water jugs. He is wearing blue canvas slippers.

I learn he is from one of the outlying pueblos in the mountains, that he makes this journey once a week to collect water for his wife from this particular fountain. He tells me this is *la funta del Santa Teresa . . . muy espíritu.* His wife is especially devoted to Santa Teresa de Avila. She believes this water restores the spirit and all manner of ailments. He invites me to drink the water with him.

I watch him walk carefully over the uneven cobbles and cannot begin to guess his age. He is a small and handsomely weathered man. He lifts his weary legs over the steps of the fountain, stoops down and then with great deliberation begins to fill each bottle. He fills one with about an inch of water, shakes the bottle then pours it out, filling it the second time as he sits down on the stone ledge above the spout. The old man enjoys several sips, wipes his mouth with the back of his hand and fills it again.

Joining him from below, I cup my hands below the running water and drink.

The old man gestures to one of the two bottles he has just painstakingly filled. It rests on the ledge like a prism separating lights the sun shines through.

At first, I do not understand. Perhaps he is offering me another drink?

Gracias, pero no.

He persists.

¿Para mí?

He nods. He hands me one of his bottles. I hardly know what to do. The old man had walked so far for this water. What will his wife say when he returns home to the mountains with only one bottle? How to receive this gift? What can I give him in return? I hold the jug of water close and feel its refreshment even against my skin.

Gracias, señor, para tu regalo.

De nada.

The old man nods and smiles and slowly shifts his weight on his right hand to ease himself up. He bends down and puts the other bottle in his bag.

After he is gone, I look back toward the fountain. "For tears gain everything; and one kind of water attracts another...."

In the Hollow That Remains

BARBARA HURD

⁊ⵔ

Go inside a stone.
That would be my way.

CHARLES SIMIC

On a recent December day I found myself squeezed into a cleft in
350-million-year-old limestone, trying to remember the final lines of
Charles Simic's poem. Just an inch from my nose, a small circle of
wet rock glowed in the light of my headlamp. Above me, the fissure
narrowed into darkness. I felt as if I were inside a gash whose skin at
the top had healed over, sealing me in at the bottom. I could swing
my light up, watch its small beam skim over ancient walls, wrinkled
and creased, like ocher-brown muscle turned to stone. Here at
the bottom, I kept my body turned sideways in the cleft, shoulder
blades pressed against the back wall. To move, I had to inch one foot
slowly to the left, shift my weight to it, bring the other foot along, resist the urge to turn ninety degrees and stride ahead, an urge that, if
heeded, could get me seriously wedged in stone sixty feet under the
earth, two thousand feet away from the cave entrance. I took a deep
breath, felt my upper body expand against the walls in front of and
behind me, remembering that I love Simic's poem because it asks

me to imagine space inside an object I'd thought of as only solid, impenetrable.

I'm clumsy in a cave. And nervous. My first attempt at caving ten years ago began in inspiration and ended in terror. I'd been teaching creative writing at an environmental camp for middle school students who were scheduled to take a field trip to a nearby cave. For two days before the trip, I primed them with stories about Mohammed in the cave, Plato's cave, why caves so often symbolize rebirth. It's a hidden space, I told them, an unexpected, inscrutable space. Shy things live in there, eyeless salamanders, albino fish, a prophet's epiphanies. I decided not to suggest to them that going into a cave might be like going inside one's own mind, crawling around in the pitch-black, nook-crannied labyrinth of the human psyche. Nor did I anticipate trouble. I didn't mention claustrophobia or the guide's warning that we'd need to belly-squirm down the initial tight passage. We were all outdoors lovers, and on the day of the expedition, we fastened the chin straps of our helmets in anticipation and lowered ourselves into the muddy mouth of the cave. One by one, the kids dropped to their knees, lay down on their bellies, and disappeared headfirst down a dark chute. Of the two guides, three instructors, and dozen students, I was the only one who couldn't do it.

I tried. But lying on my belly just inside the two-foot-high chute, pushing with my toes, I felt something moving toward me. Not just stone, but something else: the Mack truck that barreled into my cousin's car moments before his death, as if I'd been in that silent car with him, windows rolled up, both of us speechless as an impossibly large pair of headlights, steel bumper, and grille loomed into the side-view mirror, bore down on our watery bodies of burnable flesh, only I wasn't there, I was here in a dark tunnel and couldn't see what I felt, knew only that I was about to be flattened by the thing that moves inside stone, the thing that was hurtling down that tiny tunnel toward me, who was by now scratching and clawing my way backward, out of the mouth, into sunshine and fresh air.

Claustrophobia? Maybe, though as a child, I'd loved hiding in closets, under beds, under attic eaves, inside the three-by-three-foot toy box my father had made out of plywood and painted red. Hallucinations? Maybe. For years, I had no explanation of my cave terror and still don't.

But slowly I tried again. Something drew me, some curiosity about that unexpected terror and a lifelong love of stones. As a child, I'd created endless small-stone dramas in the woods behind our house, built hospitals for injured stones, performed surgery on them, nursed them back to health. In college, I signed up for two semesters of geology, mostly because I'd heard that in the labs you got credit for rubbing and licking stones. I love geodes and the rock exposed when road-building crews dynamite away the side of a mountain—anything that lets me look at what's been concealed for thousands of years. How could I let one afternoon of terror keep me from the ultimate intimacy with stone: to go inside it? I wanted to try caving again, and so I started in commercial places like Howe Caverns, their interiors sidewalked and brightly lit, spangled with dripping stalactites so fabulous you can almost forget you're inside a mountain. And later in an easy "wild" cave in nearby West Virginia, and then, on that recent December day, in a winding, deep, undeveloped cave under Laurel Mountain in southwest Pennyslvania.

Like Simic, I'm drawn to both stones and hidden places, the not-so-obvious rifts, the unexpected gaps and niches, especially the ones created by some force, physical or emotional, that has moved through and removed the insides, hollowed out the interior matter, left a space behind. Not just caves, but excavated city lots, littered and graffitied; woodpeckered trees; the lowland after the beaver dam breaks; the self after loss. There's a Tibetan word *shul*, meaning the hollow that remains after something has moved through. Buddhist monks use the word to refer to the path of emptiness, the way that opens up when one stops clinging to dogma. In Yiddish, *shul* means temple, a place to pray and to learn.

On the day I was squirming around under Laurel Mountain, I wasn't, of course, thinking about Yiddish or Tibetan words. I was exploring caves, not out of any spiritual seeking, but out of my wish to not be afraid of what I love. Mostly I was curious. And then tired. Two hours into those limestone fissures, I asked the rest of the small group to go on without me. I knew from the map that they would have to retrace their steps, that I could rejoin them on the return trek. Not only did I need to rest, but I also needed the stillness of just sitting and not fretting over where to place my foot, my fingers, how to clamber up and over a boulder I could see only in fragmented light as I swung my headlamp over it. The group disappeared down a passageway and I sat down, leaned against a stone wall, took a deep breath, and turned off my lamp.

Deep inside a cave, there's absolutely no light. You squint, hold your hands up to your face, wait for your pupils to dilate. Nothing happens. No glimmer, no pale outlines, no softening of a darkness so palpable you feel as if you ought to be able to wring it, wrest from it a beam or two of light. Total blackness. You wave your hand in nothingness, sure your fingers are setting off ripples of darkness, that your hands are leaving behind them a V-shaped wake of the less-dark. Without landmarks or skymarks, you begin to lose your bearings. You pick up a rock, consider hurling it toward the last wall you saw, consider how you'll feel if it doesn't thunk, but instead sails noiselessly and forever through the silence of an abyss at whose edge your backpack teeters, how it could be you're not halfway between Mill-stream Passage and Sleepy Rock at all, but somewhere else equally immense, sunless, moonless. You put down the rock.

I wish I could say that silent darkness moved me to some instant insight. That I suddenly understood why Buddhists prize emptiness. But what mattered was that nothing dramatic happened. The memory of my previous terror, the visions of my cousin's death, brushed faintly through me and triggered an almost imperceptible moment of anxiety. I flipped my light on, looked around, turned it off again. Stillness. It was as if those events had happened to another me. It became, in fact, oddly peaceful in that niche two thousand feet inside a limestone mountain. I became very conscious of invisible space. The limestone cracks gouged out by acidic water so many millions of years ago, the cavern walls inching back, the stone hollowed out. And some space in me opening up—what happens, perhaps, when fear unclenches its fist, uncurls its fingers, opens the palm wide. Room. An underground recess full of nothing.

Until footsteps and a small light approached and a voice in the dark said he, too, needed to rest and did I mind? Although he was apparently one of the group, and, like me, too tired to continue, I couldn't picture which man this was. The one in khaki overalls? The guy with wire-rimmed glasses? I saw his tiny beam go off, heard him drop his pack, settle himself on the cave floor. For a few minutes neither of us said a thing. And then, with no introduction, he told me he'd once been frozen to the deck of a navy ship in the early sixties, that they'd had to chip the Arctic ice from around his body, that he'd permanently lost all feeling in his right nostril. From there to his various jobs, the vagaries of his long marriage, the indulgences and difficulties, gestures of courage or supplication.

"I'm with my son on this trip," he told me. "We used to cave together often. Maybe this'll be good for us." His voice was soft, with none of the guilt of confession, nor the neediness of bravado. It didn't feel so much as if he were unburdening himself, hauling secrets out of deep hiding, sharing them, trembly voiced, with a stranger he knew he'd never see. It was more as if I were sitting inside his secrets. And then he inside mine, my small moments of bravery and shame, romances and job disappointments, the time when I, disillusioned by college, lied to my parents and left campus to ride a bus for ten days with only clean underwear and a few dollars in my pocket. It was more than the ease of talking to a stranger in the dark. It was as if the fissures and folds of our minds had slipped outside, become a part of the cave's cool interior, a place where we both could talk and listen carefully. Something about all that invisible space elicited an interaction that lacked agenda or charge, until finally even the very personal became, oddly, neither his nor mine, became simply the acknowledgment of human foibles and the occasional thought: *Ah, that too.*

In spite of the weight of some things we said, there was nothing weighty about anything we said, nothing intense about our conversation. The drama of our lives grew lighter, became no big deal. Picture a watercolorist diluting an intense indigo sky, adding water, more water. The sky lightens, fades from deep blue to pale blue, gets larger and more open, less threatening. Our words floated out into the dark and disappeared. On and on we went, the tedium of trivia and fatigue, of fear, his despair the day they diagnosed Parkinson's disease, the pain of my habitual reserve.

I surprised myself. I'm usually fairly private, certainly vigilant about solitude, famous (or infamous) among my friends for protecting my time alone. Selfish even. And yet there I was sixty feet below the earth's surface, my intention to settle into the great stillness of a cave broken by an invisible stranger with whom I sat, cross-legged and contented. The minutes, the half hours, slipped by. We kept talking. He said he could see my aura. Imagine it? I asked. No, *see* it, he said. It was pitch black in there. In other circumstances, I might have grown skeptical, bored, irritated at his intrusion, chagrined by my own admissions. But inside the stone fissure, those usual, easy reactions seemed to evaporate, dissolve in the darkness. It wasn't apathy or indifference I felt, but, curiously, a *dis*passionate interest in what we were saying. There seemed to be plenty of time, an eternity, in fact. And a growing awareness of tremendous room. This was the irony which, in retrospect, interested me first: it was spaciousness, not claustrophobia, that I felt inside that stone cave. And the spaciousness was not just physical but psychic as well. Was there something about that ancient, mostly undisturbed space, that *shul*, that made such largesse, such generous attentiveness, possible? The man and I were anonymous, invisible to each other, almost disembodied. The only sense we had of the other's place in the world—what position, status, what class we usually occupied—was rudimentary. We knew only that we happened to be in that cave at the same time. Everything else seemed interesting but mildly irrelevant, as if such a space unnamed us, made us any two humans paused within the normal pleasures and troubles of their lives.

A few weeks earlier I'd attended the annual conference of the National Speleological Society, wandered around a huge parking lot full of vehicles with bat bumper stickers, had coffee with some cavers. I'd asked a group of them what the draw was. Why crawl into such dark places? It's the great equalizer, they told me. Only one thing matters in there, and it's not your job, nor your looks, which nobody can see anyway, not your degrees nor the speed of your Internet access. Everybody enters a cave dressed in rough overalls and hard hats, boots with good tread and gloves. You can study the others, try to get a sense of body shape and maybe age by limberness or lack of it. But that's about it. You could be inching on your behind down a scrabbly slope in the mostly dark next to the Queen of England and you'd never know it. The only thing that matters in a cave, they told me, is your ability to stay calm in dark spaces.

Later, that afternoon, standing in the convention's art gallery, I studied a drawing titled *Cave beneath Mt. Virgin*. It's dark in that cave, too, except for a section of interior wall, which the artist had stippled platinum and pearl, a band of luminosity above a woman who stretches, naked, on the cave floor. The edge of her body glows orange. A woman stood next to me, both of us admiring the work. "Are you a caver?" I asked. "Yes," she answered. I asked her why and she told me a story about her addictions to drugs and alcohol, and about a friend who'd been killed in a cave. She'd felt such despair and such anger—why would anyone risk his life rappelling into the utter blackness of a sixty-foot well in old rock? His death compelled her to make her first trip into a cave in England. It turned her life around, she said. Instantly. I looked at her. Something about going into all that darkness, she struggled to explain. I'd heard cavers insist that anyone who's not comfortable in a cave is afraid of her own mind, that without the trappings and markers of our above-ground lives, the only thing left is the mind, and most of us aren't easy there. I told her about my own first cave terror. Perhaps it hadn't been claustrophobia or hallucinations at all, but a fear of empty space, the potential that absence holds, some inkling that those are inner spaces too. Robert Frost knew it: "I have it in me so much nearer home / To scare myself with my own desert places." The woman tried again to explain, but soon fell silent. Coffee was brewing on a table behind us; somebody was making change at the cash register. The question I really wanted to ask her was one I couldn't quite articulate, and even if I could, I knew she wouldn't be able to answer. I bought the artwork and left the gallery.

The ineffable is, by definition, what words can't quite say. It's

what silence is for. When we could hear the rest of the cavers returning, the man and I grew quiet. I heard him stand up, heard the rustle
of nylon as he shouldered his pack. By the time the others' lights
bounced off the walls and ceiling and their boots mingled with ours,
he'd melted back into the group. I didn't look for him afterward,
all of us out in the gray December day, unfastening our helmets
and wiping the mud from our pants. It would have been wrong, a
violation, as if the intimacy we'd had couldn't immediately be transported above ground. Suddenly shy, I pulled the hood of my sweat-
shirt up and headed for my car.

Hearing this story later, a friend wondered if the man's coming
back to sit with me had been motivated by something other than fatigue. A subtle flirtation? That hadn't even occurred to me. I'd had
no sense of intent, felt none of the teasing or testing of seduction.
Had I been too trusting? When all those markers that usually help
determine our behaviors with another are absent, how do we gauge
one another? What remains to guide us? At first, maybe nothing. Or
fear of nothing. Maybe too much innocence. That last time, under
Laurel Mountain, I wasn't afraid. Instead, it was as if that dark invisible cave-space invited the man and me to relax our boundaries, to
expand.

I think now of the troglodytes, permanent cave dwellers, which
have no need for color protection deep inside the earth and are,
therefore, often albino, almost transparent. Like the eyes of many
cave creatures, those of the Kentucky cave fish have degenerated; the
fish is blind. But its pale body is studded with vibration receptors,
tiny sensors that can detect even a slow human hand dipping into
the water. Ghostlike, the fish darts away. Cave crickets and beetles, a
whole community of pale, blind creatures relying on extra-long feel-
ers, their sensitivity to one another's vibrations.

No, I told my friend, the man wasn't flirting. I may have been unable to see, may have been literally blind to his intentions, but my other senses were highly tuned and we were, for that brief time, not the parrying, sexual selves we so often bring to human interactions. Perhaps such space, hollowed out and dark, a kind of rarefied air, allows for presences more limpid, diaphanous, magnanimous, out of which emerge a lot of attentiveness, empathy, quiet voices, and highly tuned ears in a vast underground space.

What happened in there? I wondered later. Nothing, really. No terror, no startling revelations, no new friendship. A momentary connection with someone I'll never see again. And an unexpected sense of spaciousness. "Nothing happens?" the Spanish poet Juan Ramón Jiménez asks. "Or has everything happened, / and are we standing now, quietly, in the new life?"

Though for me it was an actual cave, a fissure in ancient stone, that precipitated that sense of spaciousness, that's not the only way to become aware of it. Loss can do it too, hollow you out, leave you, like an old stone, riddled with invisible caverns. The only ghost I've ever seen came in the shape of a dog. A week earlier, a good friend had died, unexpectedly. There were things we'd needed to say to each other and hadn't. It was Christmastime, the streets and stores decked out, everywhere the flush of plenty, abundance, and inside me this stunned silence, a saber-shaped absence I felt in my body as danger, grief like a weapon I could wound myself with if I moved too fast in any direction. The atmosphere thins in sorrow time. Things that had seemed centrally important a week earlier floated toward my peripheral vision, disappeared. Everything seemed suddenly fragile, less solid. Among his friends, his children, his wife, a sudden intimacy, our boundaries collapsing as we hung onto each other.

A week after his funeral I woke in the middle of the night to hear chains rattling outside. From the window, I saw an alabaster blur circling the lilac tree at the corner of the field. I pulled on boots and went outside. The moon was full, the night sky bright with stars, the ground frozen under a foot of snow. A still night of silver and shadows and a pure white dog, his chain wrapped and wrapped around the base of the lilac.

I live in the woods, miles from town, and I know the two dogs who occasionally stop by on their treks along this ridge. I'd never seen this one before. He stood, neck trussed tight to the tree, and wagged his tail. I let him smell my palm and then I took his collar and we walked slowly around and around the tree, unwinding the chain. I was half asleep, not thinking about anything. I held on to him and walked in circles, each one a little wider than the last. Three times around, four. And then I wanted to keep going, to keep unwrapping his by-now-unwrapped chain, let him keep expanding the circle, making the orbit larger and wider, tracing an invisible, elliptical path through the woods, across the cornfields, down into the valley, back up through the woods, each orbit more far-flying than the last, the moon circling overhead, a dog at the end of a tether that grew longer and longer until he'd take off, some kind of airborne ghost-dog that would keep tugging the circumference of grief outward.

My boots crunched in the moonlit snow as I removed the chain. Untangled, the dog hesitated. And then he turned and loped across the yard, into the woods, and was gone.

I've never seen him since. How to explain all this? It was an actual dog. I went out in the morning and looked at his paw prints. In the spring, I watched the bark on the lilac close over the gashes. I have no idea to what world, if any, my friend had gone, whether he'd sent the dog to me, whether the dog was somehow his spirit. What I do know is that the dog and I acted out some silent drama that night. Neither of us said a thing. We moved together around a tree, and at the end of his tether the world billowed outward and somehow I felt I was untangling my own grief, knew that this silent, spiral-out ritual in the middle of a wide December night did more to help me let him go than did the funeral mass, the poems of tribute we wrote, the nights of reminiscing. The dog appeared on a night when I'd felt emptied by grief, and our movements, mundane as they were, took on the feel of ritual, became ecstatic, not in the joyful sense, but in the original sense of the word: taken out of one's place, taken to a different place. A larger place, a *shul*, in which a dog appeared.

You wait in the dark, in the blank absence, the void, and sooner or later, something appears, begins to take shape, something that could not have come into anything other than absence. Something, in fact, that needs absence first in order to have form later. In *The Dream and the Underworld*, James Hillman says that "dimension sensed as loss is actually the presence of the void. . . . Here in depth there is space enough to take in the same physical world but in another way." A voice in the cave. A white dog.

—

Or stalactites. At Luray Caverns in Virginia, I entered underground rooms bejeweled in cave pearls and cave orchids, the exquisite white lace of aragonite, rooms lit up like palaces and hung with millions of stalactites. The process begins in a limestone mountain reamed out by water. It begins with blank walls, bare ceilings, a newly opened space in the dark. If it's a wet cave then, for thousands of years, water drips into the emptiness. Millions of drops, each one seeping through the cave roof and dangling from its ceiling. If it hangs there long enough, it releases its carbon dioxide, which causes calcite to be deposited in a tiny ring at the very point where the drop touches the ceiling. Then another drop of water seeps through, drips through to the bottom of the ring, pauses, deposits another tiny calcite ring. What grows, then—all those fantastic shapes, all that dripping festoonery of stalactites and flowstone, thousands of burnished soda straws—requires, first, the cave's hollowing-out, and then centuries of dripping, the tiny bits of mineral left behind. In the midst of Luray's lit-up fantasia, it's hard to remember that beginning. But if you step off the path, peer into a side chasm where formations haven't grown, you won't forget you're underground in an ancient hole. You'll see only rough stone, uninterrupted blankness. Back on the main walkway, you'll see how all the now-decorated main caverns were, once, just slits in stone, how the walls inched back and back, how for thousands of years there was only an empty cave, full of dank air, the slow dripping of water.

Not even the splendor of the forms can obscure the original hollow. I want to remember this, to pay attention to the lull between emptiness and form. I want to watch the mind leaning across a blank space, reaching for a story, artifice, something, anything, to complete the metaphor. I wonder if it's possible to pause that leap, to imagine that inscrutable space the mind leaps *over*. What kind of training or discipline would it take to linger for a few moments in that blank space, image-absent and unfilled? Could I see in slow motion how a drop of water dangles? or how grief can change shape, lighten a little?

⌣

How hurt can too. A couple of years ago, I sat in a chair at the edge of the Thar Desert in India, not far from the Pakistani border. I'd been traveling with a lover who had just disclosed something that made me want to walk away, far away, out into the desert, to just keep walking, across that flat, dry expanse. It was twilight. Someone brought us cups of chai, wanted to know if we wanted music. No, I said. I wanted nothing but the nothingness of the desert. I got up out of my chair, headed away from the small village, the dancers, the decorated camels, walked in the soft sand, the small grains working their way into my shoes. The desert drew me as surely as if it were a magnet and my body a collapsing stack of iron shavings. I kicked at anything, spat out a searing attack to the empty dunes. I wanted to pound something—his head, perhaps. The desert that evening stretched everywhere, its sands of gritty buff strangely lit beneath a high ceiling of lusterless dusk. I clomped one foot after another after another into the sand, which shifted just slightly. But nothing else happened. The wind didn't gust, the Pakistanis didn't come roaring over the border, I didn't feel fortified by the satisfaction of being the one so clearly wronged, and no one from the village came to bring me back. Nothing happened. When I turned around, I couldn't even see my tracks. Everything seemed swallowed up in the vastness, the endlessness of sand, that ancient Indian sky. And finally the need to lash out in revenge lessened. I didn't have to yell or sulk or grab the first flight home. It wasn't that the hurt lifted but that there was, out there in the desert, more room for hurt, and so it didn't press so hard. That familiar sense of needing to explode with emotion eased, and it had to do, I think now, with not feeling so confined, so squeezed by, so dense with hurt. Plenty of room in a desert to feel what you feel, and plenty of time to decide what to do.

The next year I was back, farther north, where three friends and I traveled up the Ganges River, almost to its source, to find a Hindu holy man. At a ceremony the night before, a priest had pressed sandalwood into our foreheads, chanted, thrown sacred leaves into the river in the names of our children. Drums pounded, bells clanged, the village chanted. We took off our shoes, offered rupees and scarves, spent the night huddled in bed under blankets, listening to the Ganges and went groggily the next morning to the holy man's hut. I confess that I have forgotten or didn't understand most of what he said. I do remember the light-headedness at 11,000 feet, the craggy Himalayas rising even higher around us, the cold, the noise of the river, glacial white, the tidiness of his tiny hut, his lively, piercing eyes, and a single image he offered in the midst of a rambling two-hour talk: the heart, he said softly, is the only real temple. Worship there. Everything else is distraction.

And, weeks later, Sunithi, an elderly Indian woman to whom I'd told the desert story, said to me, "The heart, you know, is the widest secret space. That's where the spirit is free." She wrote *Guhaiya* in my notebook, the Sanskrit word for secret space. *Guhaiya*, which sounds like *Go here*. Everything else is distraction? I love India for its cow-jangling, horn-honking, sari-swaying excess, its lavish moon palaces and plumed elephants, the elaborate, erotic carvings on its temples. "Yes," Sunithi said, showing me a Hindu temple's exterior, its evocative stone figures. But the farther into the temple you go, the less elaborate the carvings. The innermost sanctum is always dark and unadorned. Like the human spirit, she explained. *Guhaiya*. The heart is a *shul*?

—

I don't wish to imply that a fleeting and delicate awareness of spaciousness is a gift of the cave, death, the Indian deserts, or Himalayas. We stumble into our own hollowed-out interiors just by getting up and going to work every day, just by trying to stay reasonably alive. There are plenty of caverns inside our psyches; places that have been emptied by grief and the crevice expand, become the space between planets. The viscera of absence calls us to grope where we can't see, where the normal constraints, habits, identities, and the definitions by which we live might lift, dissolve momentarily, leave us in enormous space. Here the imagination twists and searches, fumbles, gets ready to say what we can't quite see. We stand in the absence, in the clearing, the hollowed-out place and discover, not wisdom or enlightenment, but spaciousness. Room. A *shul*.

Acknowledgments

I owe a huge debt of thanks to my research assistant, Roberta Richards, for her crucial work not only in searching out fine pieces of writing for me, but also in doing the tedious and exacting job of securing permissions for *Breaking Free*. Roberta has a fine literary eye as well as a penchant for detail, a rare combination of skills. She gave me cheerful and unfailing support throughout this project. It would not be an overstatement to say that without Roberta's participation, this book would not have been possible.

Two writer friends, Brian Doyle and Joanne Mulcahy, were especially helpful in suggesting some wonderful contributors for this book. Joanne also made insightful suggestions about my own essay, as did Katie Radditz and Dianne Stepp. Because of the close reading and critique of these three friends, my essay evolved into a much finer piece than my original effort. Amy Caldwell, my editor at Beacon Press, suggested editorial changes that improved my introduction. Amy also has been a dependable and encouraging presence during the months I spent putting this book together.

I am grateful to Jan Larson, my secretary, who patiently made multiple copies of the manuscripts I had chosen, and encouraged me with her positive energy and her caring.

I also wish to thank the members of my congregation at First Unitarian Church here in Portland for acknowledging and supporting my understanding that writing and editing is an important part of my call in ministry.

Contributors

ISABEL ALLENDE is a Peruvian novelist and author of children's fiction who has won many international literary awards. Some of her best-known works of fiction are *The House of Spirits, Of Love and Shadows,* and *Eva Luna.* She presently lives and works in San Rafael, California.

MAYA ANGELOU has written novels, short stories, plays, screenplays, and poetry. She is perhaps best known for her memoir *I Know Why the Caged Bird Sings.* Born in 1928 in humble circumstances, she has become one of the most honored writers of her generation, having received fifty honorary degrees from various institutions. She now makes her home in Winston-Salem, North Carolina.

SANDY BOUCHER has pioneered the study of Buddhism and women. She was a fellow at the MacDowell Colony and won a grant from the National Endowment for the Arts. She is a founding member of the Feminist Institute in Berkeley, California, a teacher of writing workshops, and a leader of Buddhist retreats for men and women. Sandy lives and works in Oakland, California.

YVONNE MOKIHANA CALIZAR is a writer and teacher living in Kuliouou Valley, on the east side of Oahu, Hawaii. She has worked with colleges, corporations, and community groups in Washington State and throughout the Pacific Northwest and Hawaii, fostering multicultural sensitivity and integrating Hawaiian culture and language. Calizar has written and published several books, a collection of poetry, and many magazine articles.

BABA COOPER came out as a lesbian at age fifty-one. She is the author of *Ageism in the Lesbian Community* (Crossing Press, 1987) and *Over the Hill: Reflections on Ageism Between Women* (Crossing Press, 1988).

M.F.K. FISHER was a prolific author as well as an actress, scriptwriter, poet, and composer. Fisher was the recipient of many awards and served on two presidential boards. For over twenty-five years she was a visiting professor at various universities. She died in 1992 at the age of eighty-four, of Parkinson's disease.

CHINA GALLAND has worked as a wilderness guide and university lecturer, and is a scholar of comparative religion. She is the founder and director of the Images of Divinity Research Project in Berkeley, California, and lectures widely on the topic of the divine feminine. Her highly praised first book was *Longing for Darkness: Tara and the Black Madonna*.

ALMA ROBERTS GIORDAN was born in 1917 in Watertown, Connecticut. She married Robert Giordan, an artist, and they have one daughter, Nancy. Giordan continues to live and work in Watertown, Connecticut.

ELLEN GLASGOW received many honors during her career as a writer of historical fiction, including honorary doctorates of literature from the University of North Carolina, University of Richmond, Duke University, and College of William and Mary. She won the Pulitzer Prize for her novel *In This Our Life*. She died in 1945.

VIVIAN GORNICK was nominated for the National Book Award in 1974 for *In Search of Ali Mahmoud: An American Woman in Egypt* and in 1997 was nominated for *The End of the Novel of Love: Critical Essays*. A writer of social commentary and women's studies, she lives and works in New York City.

GERMAINE GREER, a native of Australia, received her PhD from Cambridge in 1967. She has written in the fields of literary criticism and history, but is best known for her work in women's studies. Greer has taught in Australia, England, and the United States. At the present time she makes her home in Tuscany, Italy.

SUSAN GRIFFIN is a writer of both poetry and nonfiction and is presently working on her first novel. Her groundbreaking book *Woman and Nature* was published in 1978. Among other honors, Susan was given a National Endowment for the Arts grant and also a Malvina Reynolds Award for cultural achievement. She is a peace and justice activist and lives and works in Berkeley, California.

BARBARA HURD is a writer and educator teaching creative writing and composition at Frostburg State University in Frostburg, Maryland, where she lives and works. She was a finalist for the Annie Dillard Award for nonfiction in 2001.

ERICA JONG has written children's books, essays, novels, poetry, and social commentary. She studied at Barnard College and at Columbia University and describes herself as a "left-leaning feminist" politically and a "devout pagan," religiously. She has received many awards for her writing, including the American Academy of Poets Award in 1963 and a National Endowment for the Arts Fellowship, 1973–74. She makes her home in New York City.

AUDRE LORDE is known for her works of poetry, memoir, and essay, especially her writing on women's issues and race relations. Lorde received National Endowment for the Arts grants in both 1968 and 1981 and was a National Book Award Nominee for poetry in 1974 for *From a Land Where Other People Live*. After courageously battling cancer for many years, she died in 1992.

KATHLEEN DEAN MOORE is an essayist who writes about our cultural and spiritual connections to wet, wild places in such books as *Riverwalking: Reflections on Moving Water* and *Holdfast: At Home in the Natural World*. Her newest book is *The Pine Island Paradox*. Her essays have appeared in a wide range of magazines, including *Orion*, *Audubon*, and the *New York Times Magazine*. Moore is Distinguished Professor of Philosophy at Oregon State University. She lives on the rainy side of the Cascade Range in Corvallis, Oregon.

JOANNE B. MULCAHY teaches and directs the Writing Culture Summer Institute at The Northwest Writing Institute, Lewis and Clark College, in Portland, Oregon. She is the author of *Birth and Rebirth on an Alaskan Island*, a biography of an Alaska Native healer. Her essays have appeared in numerous journals and anthologies, including *The Stories That Shape Us: Contemporary Women Write About the West* and *Resurrecting Grace: Remembering Catholic Childhoods*.

GRACE PALEY has written novels, short stories, poetry, and essays. She has been honored with a Guggenheim Fellowship in fiction, a National Council on the Arts grant, and many other awards and grants. Paley was a National Book Award nominee and a Pulitzer Prize finalist, both in 1994, for *The Collected Stories*. She lives both in New York City and Thetford Hill, Vermont.

FLORIDA SCOTT-MAXWELL was born in Florida in 1883 and educated mainly at home. At sixteen she went on the stage; at twenty she began another career, writing short stories. She married and went to live in Scotland, where she raised her children and wrote plays. At fifty she began yet another career as an analyst, studying under Carl Jung. At eighty-two, living alone, she kept a private notebook in which she recorded her responses to growing old; it has been published as a kind of wisdom literature.

MARILYN SEWELL is the senior minister at the First Unitarian Church in Portland, Oregon, where she has lived for the past twelve years. She also works as a writer, an editor, and a social activist. Her first book, a collection of women's poetry entitled *Cries of the Spirit*, was named one of the Best Books of 1991 by *Library Journal*.

ALIX KATES SHULMAN is known chiefly for writing novels and children's fiction. She has twice won an outstanding book citation from the *New York Times*. She was a MacDowell Colony for the Arts fellow, a Yale University fellow of Saybrook College, and she received a creative writing grant from the National Endowment for the Arts. Shulman has been a visiting writer in residence at various sites over the years and now lives and works both in New York City and in Long Island, Maine.

ANNICK SMITH has worked as an independent filmmaker and producer, an arts administrator and director, and a freelance writer.

She has won several major awards for scriptwriting, including first prize at the Sundance Film Festival and the Neil Simon Award, both for *Heartland*. She also writes short stories and nonfiction. In addition, Smith is a community organizer and an environmental worker. She lives in Bonner, Montana.

JUDITH SORNBERGER has published several collections of poetry, including *Open Heart, Judith Beheading Holofernes*, and most recently *Cones of Light*. Her poems and essays have appeared in journals such as *Prairie Schooner, Calyx, California Quarterly, Tiferet, Potpourri*, and *The Women's Review of Books*. Judith lives in Mansfield, Pennsylvania.

GLORIA STEINEM is widely known as a feminist activist. She was a Woodrow Wilson International Center for Scholars fellow, was awarded the Ceres Medal from the United Nations, and was given the PEN Center West Literary Award of Honor in 2002. She was the cofounder and chairperson of the Women's Action Alliance and a founding member of the National Women's Political Caucus, as well as the cofounder of the Ms. Foundation for Women. Steinem is a writer and a teacher of creative writing. She lives in New York City.

SALLIE TISDALE, known for her writing on local history and health-related subjects, earned Book of the Year awards in 1986, 1987, and 1988. She received an Oregon Institute of Literary Arts award and a fellowship from the National Endowment for the Arts. She lives and works in Portland, Oregon.

DOROTHY WALL is the coauthor of *Finding Your Writer's Voice: A Guide to Creative Fiction*. Her essays and poems have appeared in *Prairie Schooner, Cimarron Review*, and elsewhere.

TERRY TEMPEST WILLIAMS writes fiction, nonfiction, and poetry, and her work emphasizes her strong interest in the natural world. She was named a Rachel Carson Honor Roll inductee and received a conservation award for special achievement from the National Wildlife Federation. Williams was awarded a Guggenheim Foundation Fellowship and a Lila Wallace-Reader's Digest Writer's Award.

Credits